Humble Pie

D0089246

Humble Pie

Musings on What Lies Beneath the Crust

ANNE DIMOCK

Andrews McMeel
Publishing

Kansas City

06 07 08 09 MLT 10 9 8 7 6 5 4 3 2

ISBN–13: 978-0-7407-5465-4
ISBN–10: 0-7407-5465-3

Library of Congress Control Number: 2005040974

www.andrewsmcmeel.com

Book design by Desiree Mueller

For the Holy Trinity of Pie Makers

—Mom, GeeGee, and Carla—

I give thanks

CONTENTS

FOREWORD

Nothing as easily [as pie] stands for everything decent, good, honest, homey and American. Some people don't eat pork. Some don't eat any meat. Some people don't ingest caffeine or alcohol. Is there anyone who, as a statement of ethics or conscience, doesn't eat pie?

—Roger Welsch

Anne Dimock believes in the power of pie: "Pie has the power to start movements and create personalities; it has made me what I am today." Now I'm a pie man myself, but after reading *Humble Pie*, I realize that compared to Dimock I'm a pie agnostic. I'm a pie for breakfast, lunch, and dinner kind of guy (and after reading *Humble Pie*, I know that Ralph Waldo Emerson agreed with me: when asked about New Englanders eating pie for breakfast, he supposedly said, "What [else] is pie for?"), but that just makes me a serious pie eater, one of millions across this land who would benefit greatly from reading this book.

For Anne Dimock, pie tells all, everything from the obituary she writes for her mom, "Mary Dimock, Pie Maker, Dead at 81," to the foolproof way to judge a man by the way he eats pie: "The next time you need to evaluate the character of a man, prepare the pie of your choice, give him an ample slice, and yourself a smaller one. This is not a sacrifice, it's strategy. Let him eat, let him talk—you watch." This is pie as feminist tool. Hint, fellas: take small bites, and whatever you do, don't dig out the filling.

Pie sustains her through the loss of her mom, her grandmother GeeGee, and her mother-in-law Carla Kingstad, who used grapefruit Kool-Aid (instead of lemon juice) to make a blueberry pie while vacationing in the Canada woods. Dimock even makes a tiered wedding cake composed of nothing but pies for her best friend's wedding. She writes, "It's the generosity of pies I want you to understand. I believe it was the pies that saved us . . . saved us to become whomever we were ultimately meant to be."

Like me, Dimock loves to eat pie, and when you finish this book you will know that she thinks our pie-making culture has gone to hell in a handbasket filled with lousy, mass-produced pies with cardboard crust and canned fruit filling. "The natural habitat for pies, [the road] has changed, shrunk, disappeared," Dimock contends, and she often finds herself on the road desperately hoping upon hope that the next pie place she comes to won't let her down; she invariably finds herself disappointed and unfulfilled. But there are a couple of places she writes about that will have me hitting the road by the time you read this. For example, the former owner of the legendary Pie Nook still bakes pies for her son's restaurant in Menomonie, Wisconsin. And who wouldn't want to go to Braham, Minnesota, where they have a pie festival the first Friday in August. In truth, according to Dimock, "Every day is pie day in Braham, Minnesota."

But what Anne Dimock truly believes in is the redemptive and majestic power inherent in making pie. "I think there is a special entrance to heaven for those who walked the Path of a Thousand Pies during their time on earth," Anne writes.

She believes that pie makers are called to a particular kind of pie when they are thirty-five, and for her rhubarb pie was it. Each kind of pie, Dimock believes, is imbued with its own cosmic meaning.

Rhubarb pie is about wisdom, apple pie is about honor, and blueberry pie is about innocence. You might notice that there is nothing in here about coconut or banana cream pie. That's because Dimock is a self-described pie conservative, pro-crust and proud of it. She believes the only true pies are double-crusted fruit pies.

Her passion is so contagious she even has me, who has never baked a pie, thinking about taking the pie-making plunge. There is even a multi-page Zen treatise on how to make a pie crust that is so mystically inspiring it should be required reading for anyone contemplating making a pie, either for a living or just for fun. According to Dimock, "The path you take to the perfect pie crust is very likely to be different from mine, but if you remember that it is a meditation as well as an object of desire, you'll be fine."

You learn about the Golden Ratio in pie baking—three to one, flour to shortening. She concludes her meditation on homemade pie with the following: "When you arrive and taste the joy you've created with a homemade pie, beautiful crust and all, you will at last understand why it is that the Buddha is always smiling." Dimock has such cultural bandwidth about pie and life in general that she seamlessly refers to David Lynch's *Twin Peaks*, Ralph Waldo Emerson, Buddha, and Carl Sagan without missing a beat, or perhaps I should say a crumb.

So go ahead, start reading *Humble Pie*. Like the best pies, you just might find yourself devouring the whole thing in one sitting. The only time you'll put it down is when you head to the kitchen to make a pie. ∿

Writer and radio and television personality **Ed Levine** is the author of *Pizza: A Slice of Heaven* and *New York Eats (More)*, and a frequent contributor to the *New York Times* Dining Section.

1
THE FIRST PIE OF AUGUST

To make an apple pie from scratch,

you must first invent the universe.

—Carl Sagan

I pull the bowl from underneath the counter. I get the rest of my equipment out—measuring spoons, cups, a pastry cutter, a knife, two forks. I get the ingredients—flour, Crisco, salt, sugar. I waver over which pans to use—the nine-inch or ten-inch, Pyrex or aluminum? Weight is important in this decision, and the Pyrex pans would add more heft, even though I like the results better when using them. These are pies that must make a thousand-mile journey on my arm and the extra weight must be justified.

I had already decided there will be two pies, and they

will be apple, and they will be large. One pie, even a large one, would not be enough. There will be twelve of us to feed. One pie might be barely enough if I could trim back everybody's appetite and be satisfied with serving slivers and not slices. But I can't be satisfied with that; it is against the generous nature of the pie itself. This is no time to stint. These are the pies that will accompany me to my mother's funeral. These are the pies meant to feed my father and brothers and sisters and cousins. In about twenty hours we will all be there, in Florida, to hail Mary and her life and speed her on to her new home. But first things first; before church, before tears, we must all have a piece of pie.

The bags are packed and the airline tickets lie across the top of a briefcase. All that's left to do is make these pies and go. Inside that briefcase is the eulogy I'm to deliver. I've written and rewritten it and I think it is okay for spoken words. But the unspoken eulogy is in the pies.

I decide to use one aluminum pan and one foil pan and pick my way through a stack to find the right sizes. How did I acquire so many of these pans? I choose two and try them out for size in the double-tier pie basket that will be my carry-on. They fit, just barely, and I must be mindful not to mound up the apples too high because each tier has a limited height. I'm like a backpacker trying to shave off ounces by whittling away at a bar of soap. I decide to reduce the number of apples I'll use by two, but only two.

The really crucial decision is what type of pie to make in the first place. August is known for a wide variety of pies—berries, rhubarb, peach, cherry—but it is a little early in Minnesota for apple pies. Early apples come to market in the middle of August, but they are softer and of a different flavor than later apples. I once made a study of which early apple was the best for pies and Paula Red was the winner. If I couldn't get some Paula Reds, I would abandon apple and make rhubarb and blueberry instead. Oh, but to have apple pies—that would be best of all!

As if by magic, my preferred-customer announcement card from a local orchard arrived in the morning's mail. The orchard would open for business in three days. But I need apples now. I telephone and speak to the answering machine: "Do you have any Paula Reds available now? I need only one peck. I'll come right over. Very important pie to make. Please call back." And someone does. Yes, the Paula Reds are ready, and if all I need is one peck she'll go out and pick them for me even though they aren't open for business yet. I go right over and get the apples. Now I can begin.

The sun sets and the air is full of warmth and dampness. Nine o'clock at night is a good time to start making pies. It is all coming back to me—the fireflies in the backyard, the creaky garden gate, the smell of tomatoes on my hands—August. The pie work always began in August and the first pie signaled the start of a massive effort, a campaign that would end more than a hundred pies later. With all my ingredients and equipment arranged before me, I begin my first pie this August.

The flour in a bowl, a little salt and sugar, stirred with a fork. The shortening next, cut into cubes, then flakes, then gravel. I settle into a familiar rhythm, a familiar purpose. I could do this with my eyes closed. My daughter is at my elbow, cranking the handle of the rotating apple slicer, a tool not available to my mother and me when we occupied a similar tableau some thirty-five years ago. The scene is overripe with nostalgia, yet more is different than is the same. Different apples, different tools, different reason for doing this. A different daughter and a different relationship. We use a lot less sugar now and the pies are better for it. It's the tradition of this that's important. It's the generosity of pies I want you to understand. ～

2
IN THE BEGINNING

Good apple pies are a considerable part

of our domestic happiness.

—Jane Austen

In the beginning, there was pie and there always would be—at least in the house where I grew up. Blueberry pie, rhubarb pie, and most of all—apple pie. Other families defined themselves through traditions of camping, holidays, or ethnic identification, but we knew ourselves by the pies we baked and ate. We had nothing else to provide family cohesion. The usual glue of church, school, community volunteer work, sports, pets, music, Little League, and Girl Scouts didn't take in my family. I don't know why.

This odd nuclear family of two parents and five children,

the first generation on both sides of parents to leave home and move away, we cut ourselves from the usual ties and free-floated through a suburban existence in the 1950s. Was that it? Perhaps the postwar euphoria carried us over harsh conditions and set us down gently—too gently—on the green grass of the private swim club. Maybe the babies that arrived at intervals of two or three years—and surely that was why it was called rhythm, five in all, me the dotted half note in the middle of the measure—were born without appreciable memory. Our rivalries and alliances fell apart at no more than a hint of something better.

I have long thought that each of us was likely a magnificent human being with charm, wit, and intelligence, a star in our own circle of colleagues and friends. But we achieved little mass as a family constellation; we were a wispy galaxy dissolving at the edges, on no discernible orbit, on nobody's celestial map.

My father, Paul, the silent scientist, the only child of an older widowed mother. My mother, Mary, younger than Paul by only a few months, talkative in the extreme. They married at an age considered old for their time but about right for ours. My older sister, Kathleen, the first and much-doted-upon offspring, smart, given to emulation of our mother. She had her own bedroom. My older brother, John, artistic and goofy. He had his own sanctum in the attic, next to the mysterious cedar closet. Then me—you will find out more about me. My younger sister, Patricia, with whom I shared a bedroom, but little else. My younger brother, Tom, musician, prodigal son, who regularly gave up his room for the grandmother who stayed five months of the year. GeeGee, my grandmother, dubbed so by the first grandchild whose enthusiastic utterance of "Grandma" got only as far as the letter "G," who lived to be ninety-nine, one source of the pie lineage. Alcoholism and mental illness made their rounds, touched some of us and not others. These are the few things about us I know; I imagine the rest.

Maybe I am too harsh. After all, we had the pies. A hot, homemade apple pie graced our table every week of my life. Sometimes twice a week. The pies were always there, like money in the bank. A dearth of good pie was a hardship I never encountered, never knew must be borne up by most folk. I believe it was the pies that saved us, saved us from a total vacuum, saved us to become whomever we were ultimately meant to be. They were very good pies. And I had one every week of my life.

The edge of the Great Swamp of New Jersey was an unlikely spot for the renaissance of pie making, but there you have it. No southern accents, no farm-wife wisdom. Just the gentle musings of suburban middle-class life. Prophets can come from anywhere, even a bedroom community of New York City. When archaeologists look back upon us, hundreds of years from now, they will see that the full flowering of Pie Maker culture really began in 1953 in Madison, New Jersey, and it began in my backyard.

Trees defined the half-acre lot and Georgian brick house we called home. The tall flowering cherry, pink beyond belief. The Japanese maple, whose slim, sturdy branches could hold children. The pink dogwood. The large maple, home to many goldfinches. The weeping willows in the back, huge and precocious. A magnolia—more pink; and a white birch clump. These I remember without any prompting.

The most famous tree in our town was the Tuttle Oak and it sat in the middle of the road just a few yards in front of our driveway. When engineers were more whimsical than they are now, they designed Prospect Street with lanes flanking both sides of the tree. They allowed the tree its own place—right in the middle of the road. A little white fence with red reflectors went around its ancient trunk. I think I became a good driver because I learned while negotiating that tree every time I went in or out of the driveway. Not all drivers did as well; some of them ended up on our front lawn, astonished to see a tree in the middle of the road.

That tree taught me how to drive, how not to let surprise derail me, and how to accommodate old, implacable beings that are not going anywhere. But the trees that played an even greater role in my life were the four apple trees in the backyard. Those trees taught me plenty, but among the lessons I absorbed was an appreciation for the magnitude of experience apples could play in one's life. Two of our trees were McIntosh, and the other two of a smaller, unnamed variety we simply called "cooking apples." The trees were already mature by the time we got there in 1953. This was before the time of routinely dwarfing fruit trees into submission. Our apple trees were tall, excellent for climbing, and the haphazard construction of a tree house. Grown to their full height, they each pumped out an uncountable number of apples. What to do with them all?

The McIntosh is the perfect apple, good for both cooking and eating out-of-hand, as orchardists say. Most apples excel in one arena or the other, but when they try to do both, they fail with mediocrity. All of our apples went for making pies, but the McIntosh we also reserved for eating. Besides the pies, we made lots of applesauce, and an occasional apple brown Betty, apple crisp, or apple fritter. We gave away bushels of apples when we could not keep up. But mostly it was the pies that claimed the biggest share of the harvest.

My mother was no stranger to pies before we made the

move from Long Island to New Jersey, the Garden State. She served her pie apprenticeship under her mother and mother-in-law and knew her way around a kitchen. What to do with all this apple bounty must have initially baffled her. The family grew in that peculiar rhythm way I mentioned before until eventually there were seven of us—eight when Grandmother GeeGee stayed. It was clear we would have to eat many apples. And in this way, my mother heard and answered her calling. She put on the mantle of pie as she would an apron; she would make many apple pies.

Before we enter into the business of making pies, let us attend to a few of those annoying housekeeping details. Let us get them out of the way and never have to mention them again. There was a world of work to do before even getting to the pies.

Among all those apples that swelled, reddened, and ripened were many that were destined for the compost heap. They either dropped before their time or way, way after, but drop they did and someone had to pick them up. I began my pie apprenticeship by picking up the fallen apples before my brother took a run with the lawn mower under the trees. This is where I first learned about division of labor by gender. In our world, the men ran the lawn mower and the women picked up the rotten apples. It was not fair and no one even tried to convince me it was. I don't think my brother enjoyed mowing the lawn, but I am sure he would have liked picking up those apples a lot less. The job fell to my younger sister and me.

The slightly sour-sweet smell from the backyard meant we were overdue in our labor. We considered ourselves fortunate if the apples were not too far gone, but that was rarely the case. The half-life of an apple on the ground is astonishingly short. Most of those apples were disadvantaged to the point of brownness and mushiness. A patina of little white dots indicated that a good crop of mold had already set in. They oozed a sticky juice that attracted yellow-jacket wasps. We screamed in horror—at the wasps, at the mess, and at our bad fortune to be girls with such a task.

We tried to pick up the apples by the still-firm side or by a precariously attached stem, any handhold to avoid contact with the rotten pulp. We ran to the wheelbarrow as fast as we could only to have our motion disturb the delicate tension. The leaking mass fell away from its shaft and splatted to the ground. We screamed a lot. We were two prissy girls, running from the wasps and the smell and this peculiar female duty. We had sly hopes that our father would soon tire of our hysteria and excuse us from the chore, but no, we still had to pick up all the fallen apples.

For what purpose? Was it for any sound reason like good orchard management, to reduce the likelihood of coddling moths or to fend off fire blight disease? No, it was just to prevent my brother from hitting one of those biological grenades with the mower, splattering the brown pulp to kingdom come. Secretly, I loved to imagine just such a punishment for him, a glorious payback for all those years I had to pick up the rot. I would pave the yard with rotten apples, then make him run a gauntlet with the mower over the wretched things, spurting the stuff back into his face until he was covered with it. Then the wasps would come. Then I'd make him lick it all off. It was so cool.

Someone came around once a year with a big truck to spray the trees. I don't know with what, but I imagine it was some sort of broad-spectrum pesticide/fungicide, a one-two, knock-'em-out combo. No childhood cancers in this family; that would come later. The trees seemed to require little more attention than to relieve their branches of their heavy burden. We had a long bamboo pole with a wire basket on the end to pick the higher apples. Like an atlatl, it extended man's reach and dominion over his food. It was a most useful tool. This was largely men's work, hunting apples to my gathering them, but occasionally I got to pluck some good ones from the branches.

The pie work was exclusively female. After the men left

the bushels of apples by the door to the kitchen, they vanished into male bastions of toolsheds, garages, and workbenches with vises. The womanly workbench was the kitchen table and our own tools were similarly off-limits to them. Until I could be trusted handling knives and peelers, my official job was to measure sugar and sprinkle cinnamon. My mother insisted that each pie contain a full cup of sugar, and although I knew that was too much, I dutifully scooped and leveled and poured oceans of sugar upon fleets of pies. She was admiral of the Good Ship Apple Pie and I her kitchen swabbie. Sometimes I would skimp on the sugar and when she caught me, she commanded, "More sugar!"—the anthem of the fifties—until each eight-inch pie crested a white cap. We must have made a thousand of them.

Perhaps this is not what one would expect for the beginning of a Pie Renaissance, but that is just how it had to start. It was up to my mother to define volume, and indeed, she created the critical mass that got the renaissance off to its start. My task has been to take out the extra sugar and put in the integrity. It's a path I still walk. Pie has the power to start movements and create personality; it has made me what I am today. And if there was any glue that held our family together, it was the glue of pie, that sweet amalgam of too much sugar, rotten apples, and yellow-jacket wasps. ∼

3

MILE 0—THE PIE RAMBLE

A hot pie cooling smells different

from a frozen pie thawing.

—Peg Bracken

A ramble is a lighthearted sort of quest. It often resembles aimless wandering, but there is a direction—it always goes toward something, never away. And there's always a destination, but it may not be the destination you first thought of when setting out. It is fueled by the same ancient hunger with no name that initiates all quests, but it takes a more leisurely, circuitous route. There is no stepwise set of directions; all tangents are welcomed and explored. A ramble is purpose with whimsy. It favors experience over instruction. It begins with an idea or memory. The Pie Ramble begins with the idea that anything lost can be found again.

The modern-day American ramble is the road trip, the urge to get in the car and drive, seeking to satisfy a hunger with no name, to scratch an itch, to fill an empty vessel. There is always a new beginning on a road trip, a fresh adventure about to unfold with every turn of the ignition key. To satisfy our American longing, we get in the car and drive.

After we've been driving for about two hours, that longing tweaks us in our stomachs and we want nothing more—and nothing less—than to stop at a café or diner for a cup of coffee and a piece of pie. This is an old idea, an artifact of our parents' and grandparents' time, and much harder to do in our time than theirs, for there is very little good pie anymore. Even if we find good pie on the road, it quickly disappears under the weight of demand. But we are hopeful and give it a try. We drive across the land at hundred-mile intervals, searching for the pie that will fill the hole in us, not fully appreciating that the car and the highways helped eradicate some of pie's natural habitat.

But there must be some left. We aren't sure where to look anymore; the small-town bakery and the diner on Main Street have closed up in favor of the big-box mall outside of town. We check guidebooks and Web sites for tips. The natural habitat for pies has changed, shrunk, disappeared. All too often, when we finally find a piece of pie, it disappoints us with the dense crust and stiff filling of the mass-produced pie. We get in the car again and drive some more. It must be out there somewhere. ∿

4
The Queen of Pies

The best of all physicians
Is apple pie and cheese!

—Eugene Field

We can get some really wretched summer weather here in Minnesota. The Land of 10,000 Different Weather Reports is known for its extremes of weather. Siberian winters, New Delhi summers, a couple of hours of a San Diego spring, and everything in between. Like how to drive in snow, Minnesotans annually forget that August will bring another level of discomfort as the dew points and temperatures race each other to new heights. Weak and flaccid, everyone walks around saying, "It's not so much the heat as the humidity" as if it were a mantra. Everybody complains a lot and retreats to air-conditioned bunkers to wait it out.

I do my share of complaining too. I forget that I was raised in this type of weather. The Great Swamp of New Jersey is located right by my hometown of Madison. The Great Swamp is a spongelike accident of geology. "Wetland" doesn't come close to describing it. It is a vast tract of low-lying swamp that has more in common with the Everglades than a prissy little pond with cattails. It's a breeding ground of mold, mildew, and mosquitoes. At night it gives off vapors and glows in the dark, raucous with amphibian life. It is never merely humid in the Great Swamp, it is sodden. You don't fry eggs on the sidewalks there in August, you poach them.

Minnesota has nothing on those steamy days of August in the Great Swamp of New Jersey. Those days were just one glass of iced tea after another. That being the time before air-conditioning was a standard feature in houses, we tried not to move around much after ten in the morning. We closed the windows, pulled the shades and curtains, and laid out the coasters for those sweaty glasses of tea. We didn't so much perspire as macerate in our own juices. It was miserable but it was our life, it didn't vary, and we got used to it.

In Minnesota you can feel that the edge of summer has burned off by the time the first apples ripen. Not so in New

Jersey, where you must commence the pie work in humidity so youthful that it promises to linger through a prolonged adolescence. But Pie Makers wear that humidity like a badge of courage. Anyone can make a pie in October—dozens of pies in October. But a Great Swamp August? That is an entirely different matter.

August brings out an unspoken competition among Pie Makers in the Great Swamp. How early could you start? How many hours at a time? How long could you last? How many pies in August? Pie Makers never ask these questions of each other, but slyly leak this information about themselves to one another in thinly veiled conversation about the pie work. Each keeps a running tab of her own pies and an estimate of her neighbors'. This is not about petty jealousies or base ambition, but rather endurance and yield, pride and admiration. Pie Makers feel awe and draw inspiration from the one among them who tops all the rest. The one who will begin on August 1 with blueberries and cherries and proceed through peaches and blackberries and onward to apple, and who doesn't stop until August 31 and will have made at least sixty pies. August is the hallmark of Pie Makers. Unequaled for versatility, volume, heat, and relentless humidity, August separates the Pie Makers from the bakers. August tests you, pushes to you to your limit, makes you stand on your own. It drives you crazy with fruit and makes your crust go bad. And the Pie Maker who emerges from the Great Swamp of New Jersey in August with the most pies is revered. And that Pie Maker, more often than not, was my mother—Our Lady of the Great Swamp, Mary Dimock, the Queen of Pies.

My mother had a mission and a system, but I never knew which came first. Was all her pie making a response to a large family and a small orchard? Or did she have this pie making life all figured out and took her time to find the right man, birth five children, and find a house with four apple trees? Once she landed in the Great Swamp of New Jersey, she might well have exclaimed, "At last! Time to get to work!"

For days at a time, our kitchen table hosted the great work of the pies. The table was actually a hollow frame door that my dad nailed legs onto. It had enough surface area to arrange eight pie pans and still have plenty of work space to peel the apples and roll out the crust. We never did more than eight pies at a time. The Queen said that the pies lost their integrity after eight, that some thresholds should never be crossed. She's right. Others approach making pies in assembly-line fashion and it always shows. Those pies lack greatness. We always crafted our pies one at a time, lovingly finished and crimped before starting the next one. That's not to say that the Queen wasn't fast and efficient—she was. She wouldn't have been the Queen if she weren't. And she had her helpers. I was always called into service during August, culling blueberries, peeling apples, measuring sugar, sprinkling cinnamon. I served out my apprenticeship during a great many Great Swamp Augusts. Our goal was to put a hundred pies in the freezer each year. And that didn't include all the others immediately baked, eaten, or given away. A hundred pies in the freezer—that sounded like money in the bank to us.

The Dimock family didn't can—we froze. The large upright freezer humming in the basement stood as a monument to our industry, thrift, and art. We stacked each drawer with unbaked frozen pies wrapped in white freezer paper and labeled by type, ready to be called into service at a moment's notice. We were never more than fifty minutes away from a hot home-made pie. A few corners of the freezer held cans of orange juice and packages of beef, but most of the space in that big humming monolith held a hundred pies, staggered and stacked to use all available space. And after a couple of those steamy pie making sessions in August, I wanted to crawl in there with them.

Eight pies at a time, more than a hundred pies a year, for decades. That's how my mother became the Queen of Pies. But the numbers don't really matter; she would have become Queen anyway, and this is why.

Our family had a special basket for carrying pies, a

legacy from my grandmother GeeGee, herself an important branch in the pie heritage tree. The basket, made of woven maple plaits, contained a divider so it could carry two pies at once and had strong, sturdy handles. The message was clear—it was nice to have pie at home every week but pies should also leave the house. The basket went everywhere—to church, to the homes of friends and relatives. My mother was a much-sought-after dinner guest because of those pies. My parents answered every dinner invitation with an offer to bring pies for dessert. I often wondered if all those hostesses first planned their menu around apple pie, then picked up the phone to call my mom.

I also wondered if my mother saw those four apple trees in the backyard as something less than work and something more than opportunity. Already married to my father for eight years when they moved to Madison and the apple trees, she must have seen that her life with him would be, well, uneventful. Those trees looming large and heavy with fruit became her ticket to a rich and fulfilling social life. She always met my father's weekly pie requirement, but then she transformed the rest of those apples into parties, gifts, covered-dish church suppers, invitations, door prizes, sick-bed offerings, and other kindnesses. People sought her out, included her in everything, and invited her everywhere. She pulled away from her moorings, the pie basket on her arm, and left the rest of us in her apple pie wake. But as her sphere widened, so did ours. The sons and daughters of the lucky adults on the receiving end of the pies became known to us, became acquainted, became friends. She was loved, and by association, so were we. Her life and ours would have been different without those trees.

Mary Dimock has slowed down a lot since her halcyon days in the Great Swamp. It's been a long time since she put a hundred pies in the freezer, but once a Queen, always a Queen. She doesn't live in the Great Swamp anymore either; she lives in south Florida, a land inhospitable to Pie Makers, for apples and rhubarb do not grow there. Whenever she visits me up here in Minnesota, she always takes a couple of pecks of fresh apples with her and makes a few more apple pies. She even uses frozen ready-made piecrusts now; at this stage of her life she has earned that right. She just passed on the pie basket to the next generation—me.

Where do the Queens of Pie go after they have rolled out their last piecrust? I think there is a special entrance to heaven for those who walked the Path of a Thousand Pies during their time on Earth. When that time comes for my mother, I imagine that she'll be borne up like another Mary on a heavenly host of pie in August. And at the exact same moment, somewhere in the Great Swamp of New Jersey, a Pie Maker will open the oven door and the heat and humidity released will cause the apples to fall from the trees. And the apples will slice themselves into a thousand pies and the pies will multiply and fly to all who need them. And everyone will know that a great soul has passed and will give thanks and reverently murmur, "Yea, she was truly the Queen of Pies." ⁓

5
RHUBARB

The knotted leaf

Unfurled to red stalk

Cleaves the earth with such happiness

—Rhubarb Pie-ku

Each Pie Maker is called to a particular type of pie. It is a deeper, more profound relationship than a favorite pie or one's specialty. It is closer to destiny or fate. If Pie Makers made totem poles, the pie they are called to would be the one they place on the top.

My mother was called to apple pie and I have been called to rhubarb. The calling might be revealed slowly, or make itself known quickly in a flash of genius, but it is never a choice. Pie Makers do not weigh and consider their calling. They do not choose among berries or stone fruits as one might choose a pair of shoes. The Pie Maker is called and that's all there is to it; she either heeds her call or not.

To be called requires a certain amount of life experience. Travel, responsibility, disappointment, joy—these are among the prerequisites. It can't be hurried or made to happen according to some timetable other than its own. The average age when Pie Makers receive their calling is thirty-five. Most of the Pie Makers in my family received their calling in their thirties. I was thirty-six when I was called to rhubarb, the same age as my mother when she was called to apple. I've known Pie Makers who got their call as young as twelve, though this is rare, and others who didn't even know they were Pie Makers until after retirement from another profession. And in at least one case I know of, a Pie Maker who always believed her calling was peach, indeed who moved to warmer climes in order to more intensely exercise her calling, learned otherwise when a brush with mortality made her realize it really was mincemeat all along. There she was, in a wreck of a car after sliding off an icy road. Her years down South left her forgetful of the vagaries of northern winter driving. At age fifty-four, Betty Ann Carlson lay pinned behind the wheel, all the pies of her life flashing before her eyes, until the Jaws of Life released her,

released her to an epiphany, to the certain knowledge that—
yes! It was mincemeat!—whereupon she quickly recovered and
moved back North to pursue and master the mysteries of the
mincemeat pie.

I heard my call in the spring of 1988. We had just
moved into a new home in Afton, Minnesota, with an eight-
month-old baby girl, moving one state over from the teeming
urban life in Madison, Wisconsin. On a parallel course that I
think of as one of Life's Great Imponderables, my mother moved
one state over from New York to a new home in Madison,
New Jersey, with an eight-month-old baby girl (me) when she
was called to apple. We were the same age at the time of our
calling and our lives would never be the same. Such splendid
constancy and connection! It happens often among Pie Makers.

And so I moved into our Afton house with its five acres
in early April, and with babe on hip I walked the yard every
day to see what might emerge from the gardens after the snow
melted. April wore on with its lion's mane and little lambie tails
waving in the breeze as I looked every day for a sign of life.
That's how April is in Minnesota, waiting for the green to
come back. Wait, wait, wait.

The first botanical specimen was unfamiliar. No sprout,
no slender blade of green, it was instead an eruption of red
tissue, a big wrinkled, rather obscene-looking knob of vegetable

flesh heaving its way out of the ground. And there wasn't just one or two of these, there were lots, all in rows. In a few weeks I saw that the monster was rhubarb and that someone before me had planted three rows of ten plants each. Thirty rhubarb plants—it still takes a while for that number to sink in.

If you don't know rhubarb, you don't know how much thirty plants is. Most families of seven get by just fine with one rhubarb plant in the garden. What was I going to do with thirty?

Flush with the romanticism of rural life, and resourceful to the point of being cheap, I decided to harvest the rhubarb and sell it. I pulled the stalks, going up one row then down the other. Each stalk fought back a little, resisting being torn from its mother. In another day I pulled them again; it grew ferociously. I pulled my back, too. I trimmed off the leaves and heaped the stalks into a small mountain to hose off the mud. I weighed and bound them into two-pound bundles. I must have had a hundred of them. It was backbreaking labor. Now I had to sell the damn stuff.

In a marketing plan that harkened back to my days selling lemonade from a card table set up in front of my house, I wrote RHUBARB on a piece of heavy cardboard and stapled it to a stake that I placed next to my driveway. And I waited. And waited. Traffic for rhubarb was light because families were smaller by then and nearly everybody had one of those seven-person-size rhubarb plants. But one lady finally came by.

"How much rhubarb do you have?"

"More than anyone could possibly want."

"Wanna bet?"

She bought all I had that day and took out an option for all the rest yet to harvest that year, and the next year too. Who knew the rhubarb business was so easy? This lady owned a bakery and coffee shop and rhubarb pie was a favorite among her customers. She couldn't grow enough to meet the demand. Hmmmmm . . . something began to make itself known—the first stirrings of the Call.

I came from one of those seven-person-size families who had one big rhubarb plant in the garden. Typically we made one or two rhubarb pies, a little rhubarb sauce, then gave the rest away to a neighbor who didn't have any. That was it until the next year. The idea that one might cultivate rhubarb as a crop was preposterous. It was a diversion, a mere trifle, something to fill in until the real pie material—blueberries, cherries, apples—came in later in the season.

With all this rhubarb abundance, I searched for recipes to use more of it. Rhubarb compote, rhubarb kuchen, sweet echoes of Minnesota's Scandinavian and German heritage. Cakes, muffins, and then, finally, a pie. I came to rhubarb the same way my mother came to apple—out of utility and thrift.

The first flush of satisfaction at taming rhubarb into a

predictable result in no way prepared me for the epiphany to come. I try to think back to the time before rhubarb. What did I ever expect from a rhubarb pie? It could not have been much, just a pleasant tart filling that could be had long before the apples ripened. A substitute was all I sought. What I found instead was profound.

If pies are where the sundry arts of life converge and form a critical mass, then it is rhubarb that provides the catalyst that sets it all in motion. The full force and power of pie comes out through rhubarb. It channels all the good that is within us and gives complete expression to the ordinary becoming the divine. Rhubarb has it all—the power to enrich, to humble, to satisfy, and to make everybody happy. It is God's wisdom and women's engineering, which are two ways of saying the same thing. Rhubarb may even be God.

Rhubarb pie has some remarkable qualities. It places everyone on an equal footing and teaches what is really important and essential in this world. It is also one of the best pies to set the stage for a reconciliation. It doesn't matter how long the feud or what it was about, rhubarb pie loosens everybody's grip just enough to work some magic. A couple of forkfuls and adversaries begin to lower their guard. An entire slice leads to declarations of mutual support and admiration. There is much to admire in a rhubarb pie: the perfect pairing of opposites—sour and sweet—and the proof that they can, and should, coexist.

My abundance of thirty rhubarb plants led me to my calling—I would go forth and perfect the rhubarb pie. I would make many rhubarb pies. It also led me to a deeper understanding of the power of all pies. The pies of one's calling will do that, whether they are cherry pies or banana cream.

What does it feel like to be called? I can't speak for all Pie Makers. Some describe the cymbal crash and flash of light of a born-again experience. Others tell of traveling down a long tunnel with a bright light at the end. For me it was a quiet knowing that I had just been given a valuable gift. What the call does to each Pie Maker is to change his or her life, and always for the better.

All of this comes from a poor, lowly plant relegated to a forgotten corner of the garden. Given the sort of renewal rhubarb is responsible for, it should come as no surprise that it needs a nutrient-rich diet. It does very well with the kind attention each year of a generous layer of compost. When I die, I want my body cremated and my ashes mixed in the compost heap. Come the next spring, I want those thirty rhubarb plants rewarded with shovelfuls of compost. Then I want everybody to have a piece of rhubarb pie.

THE SECRET TO RHUBARB PIE

I made many rhubarb pies after heeding my call in 1988, enough pies to figure out just the right formula to capture rhubarb's perfection. And because pies are meant to be shared, here it is:

"For every cup of sliced rhubarb, add ¼ cup sugar and 1 tablespoon of flour."

That's it. The secret to rhubarb pie is a simple ratio that will give it just enough sweetness to balance the sour and just enough thickening to slow the ooze. The ratio holds true for whatever size pie you wish to make.

Pie Pan Size	Cups of Sliced Rhubarb	Cups of Sugar	Tablespoons of Flour
8 inches	4 cups	1 cup	4 tablespoons
9 inches	5 cups	1¼ cups	5 tablespoons
10 inches	6 cups	1½ cups	6 tablespoons

The amount of flour may need to be reduced a little if the rhubarb is not very juicy; let experience guide you.

More secrets to rhubarb pie:

Add a little bit of cinnamon and a couple of dots of butter. I think rhubarb has great affinity with cinnamon, but others sorely disagree—like the state fair judge who lowered my score on rhubarb pie just because of the cinnamon. What does she know anyway?

There are many of you who are adamant about adding a cup or so of strawberries to your rhubarb pie, but I beg you to try one without them. You will never experience the full power of a rhubarb pie with strawberries in there. But don't do it for my sake. Do it for your own.

Straight-Up Rhubarb Pie

Crust:

Pie dough for a two-crust pie. If you don't have your own crust recipe, you can find one on page 111.

Filling:

8-inch pie	9-inch pie	10-inch pie
4 cups sliced rhubarb	5 cups sliced rhubarb	6 cups sliced rhubarb
1 cup sugar	1¼ cups sugar	1½ cups sugar
4 tablespoons flour	5 tablespoons flour	6 tablespoons flour
1 pinch cinnamon	2 pinches cinnamon	¼ teaspoon cinnamon
1 tablespoon butter (optional)	1½ tablespoons butter (optional)	2 tablespoons butter (optional)

- Preheat the oven to 425 degrees.

- Roll out the dough for the bottom crust.

- Combine the rhubarb, sugar, flour, and cinnamon in a large bowl and mix well.

- Place the rhubarb mixture in a crust-lined pie pan.

- Dot with the optional butter.

- Roll out the top crust, place on the rhubarb, trim, seal, and cut several vents.

- Bake at 425 degrees for 15 minutes.

- Reduce the heat to 350 degrees and bake 25 to 30 more minutes. Add 5 to 10 more minutes of baking time for larger pies; look for a bit of pink ooze to emerge from the vents in the crust.

6

• REST STOP •

MILE 72—ON THE ROAD

Promises and pie-crust are made

to be broken.

—Jonathan Swift

I pulled into the strip mall parking lot and parked the car. The bakery and café were in the center of the mall, an anchor, a drawing card, a destination, for the lot was nearly full and turned over frequently. It was a midsize town, a banking and transportation center for the surrounding agricultural area. There is the potential for good pie in such places.

In a way it was sort of a homecoming. I came to visit the bakery of the woman who bought my rhubarb, to sample her pie made with my rhubarb. I had never been here before; I felt like a mom who sent her child to college and was now visiting during Parents' Weekend. How is the child doing? Will I notice a change? Was this the right choice?

I sat at the counter and ordered a slice of rhubarb pie. I saw more than a dozen whole pies on the bakery shelves, and several more twirling around in a revolving dessert display. The place certainly had pies—pies to eat now and pies to take home or to the office. Customers coming and going. The signs looked good.

The waitress set the plate down before me and I beheld a slice of rhubarb pie. It sat there on its plate, still, motionless, not a drop of juice oozing from its sides. Oh dear, this doesn't look right.

And it wasn't. I could name everything that was wrong with this pie—too dense and thick, too sweet, too pale—but why put ourselves through this? The commitment to pies was admirable even if they didn't even come close to making the Dean's List. The pies were not an afterthought in this establishment; they were prominently featured, there was variety, they were made there on the premises, and the owner even sought out locally grown rhubarb. So promising, but it was hard not to go away disappointed.

I took several courtesy bites, then paid my bill. Time to move on. ᴄ∾

7

HAPPY FATHER'S DAY

A boy doesn't have to go to war to be a hero; he can say he doesn't like pie when he sees there isn't enough to go around.

—E. W. Howe

The rhubarb grew and grew. Each spring the repetitive motion of stooping, pulling, and yanking led me to curse my bounty. Not quite forty years old, how could I be too old for this? But maybe it was time to give a younger person some experience in the rhubarb business. And then along came Mark, the ten-year-old son of the neighbor two houses down.

Mark's family were friendly neighbors, with two parents and three kids, and a couple of dogs. Theirs was not the suburban lifestyle fast becoming entrenched in our little town. Theirs was more the old-time, born-again, sweat-of-the-brow, God-fearing lifestyle of several generations ago. Mark was sandwiched in between an older brother and a little sister, and the spring of his tenth year was a difficult time for his family. This close-knit family was deeply religious and it seemed that troubles rained down upon them. I sometimes wondered about the possible link between their strong Christian faith and the frequency with which it was tested. It seemed as if they wore the equivalent of a KICK ME sign on their backs: money, health, jobs, lawyers, cars—nothing went right and nothing worked the way it should. Where did their bad luck come from? Others, harsh and critical in their judgment, said they brought it on themselves. All I know is that in addition to all their problems, they couldn't get any rhubarb to grow in their yard.

The father was ill; the residual effects of polio as a youth left his body filled with pain and spasms. He was a short-haul truck driver but could not work that year. The mother took on some sales work but it wasn't enough. There was no insurance. They held occasional rummage sales to raise some money. So when Mark came around that spring asking if there were any jobs he could do for money, I hit upon the rhubarb plan.

Mark was big for his age, hefty and chunky, but his

body showed promise of being able to move refrigerators or mattresses if he had to. He had white-blond hair tightly trimmed into a buzz cut; scratches and scabs up and down his limbs; he was sweaty and smelly, with sky-blue eyes and the face of an angel. He wasn't spoiled, and he wasn't a brat or a bully, but he was annoying in a Dennis the Menace sort of way. And talkative, man, was he talkative! Whenever Mark came around it was always "why this?" and "why that?" and what did I think Jesus meant by creating wood ticks, or how come some dogs are mean and some aren't? And why do we buy more groceries than his family when there are only three of us and five of them?

I made Mark a deal. He could pick my rhubarb, cut off all the leaves, wash it, and bundle it. I'd take it to the bakery and give Mark the money for his work. It solved several problems—the rhubarb got picked, the bakery got their delivery, and I got to ease my conscience. He liked the idea and got right on the job.

For the first ten minutes he went at it with market-driven zeal. I'm sure he thought he was going to make millions. He slowed down considerably for the second ten-minute stretch, then, quickly bored, fetched his little sister to help. Off and on for two afternoons he picked his way through the thirty plants in slow motion, interrupted by occasional bursts of speed in which he saw himself as savior to his family, and always with a running commentary of the neighborhood and the challenges his family faced. The neighbor who didn't love her dog enough. The cranky boss and the mean doctor. The unfair teacher at school and the bully in his class. The crazy veteran who sat silent by his window, glaring.

Mark finally got the job done. I looked over the rhubarb patch and saw—nothing. In spite of my supervision and instruction to not pick the entire plant, each plant was picked clean. Nothing remained to show that there was ever a patch of rhubarb. It would take years to bring it back.

Mark's crop weighed in at sixty-four pounds, and at the price of 50 cents a pound, he made a whopping $32. Not bad for a ten-year-old boy goofing off on a job that should have taken him two hours at best. But Mark was clearly disappointed. I suspected he was going to turn the money over to his parents and they'd use it to buy food or pay the electric bill. His family needed so much more and Mark thought he could do it all for them—he wanted to do it all. His disappointment hung in the air, and his realization of his own limitations in the face of the terrible need still haunts me.

I inherited Mark that year. He came over every day for some attention, as well as the chance to make a little more money. I dreamed up things for him to do. He was always underfoot, more trouble than help, his smelly feet stinking up the house. I gave him a couple of dollars to play with my daughter each afternoon he came over. He would turn on the TV set and watch the vile shows that ten-year-old boys watch. This wasn't what I had in mind, but he was good at roughhousing, which was just fine for my energetic girl.

One afternoon Mark arrived looking particularly hang-dog. His father was dying, he cried dramatically. We're all dying, I silently thought, not ready to concede the point, or the afternoon, to Mark. His father was very ill and probably dying if you took the long view of death. He would be around for a while, living a difficult life. But would he be around for those events that signaled Mark's arrival upon the world? Mark sensed that he would not.

Father's Day was coming up and weighing heavy on Mark's mind. He wanted to buy something for his dad, and his dad needed so much. His dad needed a better life—deserved a better life than the one he got. Mark didn't know what to get his dad, and he didn't have very much money, which I took to be a hint. I faced up to the intimation and suggested that he make something for his dad; why, I would even help him. "What? What?" he cried. "Well, how about a pie?" It was my perpetual answer to gift giving on a budget. He wasn't sure, so I counted out all the advantages. It was something he could make. His dad probably wouldn't get another one like it. It was something that would become a part of him and of everyone else who ate it, and you couldn't say that about many gifts. And he wouldn't have to spend any money. That did it. Mark said okay and we swore secrecy and arranged to meet the next day to get to work.

Of course it was to be a rhubarb pie. I don't remember where the rhubarb came from. Was this before Mark cleaned out my patch, or was it from my own private stash, which I hoarded? Maybe I went out and bought the damn stuff, I don't know, but it had to be a rhubarb pie. But I do remember the day, a hot, humid, muggy day that is hard on your nerves and on your piecrust. Mark's job was to cut the rhubarb stalks. He cut them into carrot-stick lengths. Sent back to the counter to do the job over again, he spent two hours, cutting each stalk individually, minutely, slowly. We were way behind schedule and the piecrust was not cooperating. Bad day for making pies. The crust crumbled in my fingers as I attempted to lift it into the pan. Mark chattered on about how his sister nailed one of her fingers to a picnic table, about Ninja Turtles, about donkeys, about the receding hairline of the youth group leader at his church, about Jesus, about thunder and where it comes from, about TV shows and summer camp and whether or not he could go, about everything. Everything, except he never once mentioned his father.

I had to bring it up. "So, Mark, do you think your father is going to like this pie?"

"It's probably going to kill him," he answered, then fell silent.

I didn't bring it up again.

We finally got that pie put together and into the oven, the oven I had optimistically preheated over an hour before. Everything was sweating. The sky had that yellowish-gray cast that foretold tornado conditions. A thunderstorm paused long enough to shed its excess humidity into the already saturated air. No good wind to blow it all away, just more wet. The kitchen throbbed with sticky heat.

Then the pie was done—finally! It looked beautiful, all tan and soft brown on top with a dribble of pink juice peeking out from one of the vents. An exciting pie! It was talking as I pulled it out of the oven. It spoke of promises and mysteries and new songs to be sung. I called Mark over so he could listen.

"Do you hear it, Mark?" I asked.

"Yeah. What's it saying?"

"Shhhh. Listen."

And we did. The rhubarb bubbled and whispered, and the hot-fruit-cinnamon smell pulsed its way out through the crust. The steam, sound, and scent mingled and floated above the pie in gentle swirls, then condensed into the image of

Mark's father. The steam spoke to Mark and promised something better, some improvement, something that was going to make them all sing again. Mark spoke back to the pie, saying it was okay, that he was okay, and that he'd help and make some things better. They spoke some more, Mark and whatever it was that was in the pie. I felt like an intruder, so I stepped aside to watch, and I witnessed the boy become father to his own. The pie slowly ceased its bubbling, and the vapor slowed to soft little heaves. Mark fell silent. We put the pie in a safe place to await its official presentation, though the gift had already been given.

Later on I met Mark at the foot of his driveway. I brought over the pie, which had been cooled and secreted on my sill. We didn't talk much. He was too excited to stand there with me—he wanted to get back to his house and show off his pie. But I lingered a few moments and watched him half-walk half-run up his driveway, no longer the disappointed youth. And from within his house I heard the low murmur of wonderment as Mark presented his pie. Peace, happiness, and contentment reigned—if only for as long as the pie lasted. Lord, that family could have used a thousand pies. But this one would do, would do just fine.

Happy Father's Day, Mark. ∾

8
APPLE

Thy breath is like the steame

of apple-pyes.

—Robert Greene in *Arcadia*

Bring unto me apples,

for I am weary of Love.

—Song of Solomon

Apples have come a long way from their marble-size ancestors on the steppes of Kazakhstan. The journey from Old World to New, from sour to sweet, from puny to gigantic is a long and interesting story populated by Silk Road traders, Roman potentates, European peasants, and

American eccentrics. But we will take just a small slice of the apple's story and reflect upon the qualities that make an apple desirable, that make some better than others for pie, and why the hell the Delicious apple dominates the U.S. apple market.

Apples are part of Americans' national identity in a way no other fruit is. Maybe we embrace its immigrant heritage and hybrid vigor as a reflection of ourselves. Or perhaps the march of apple orchards east to west, courtesy of John Chapman, reinforced the myth of manifest destiny. Apples symbolize some of our strongest values: health—an apple a day keeps the doctor away; education—the shiny red apple for the teacher; family—Mom and apple pie; and the flag—as American as apple pie.

Minnesota had a cool and rainy growing season this year, and while it slowed the growth of garden favorites like corn, tomatoes, and peppers, the weather was ideal for apples. Apples are an important crop in Minnesota, and except for the box or two that gets shipped to retirees in Florida, our apples don't leave the state. Every apple grown here is spoken for by Minnesotans. Our own harvest isn't enough either; we import many times over the number of apples we actually grow here. It's the same in other states because Americans love their apples. Powerhouse apple-producing states like New York and Washington pick up the slack, and after we've exhausted the

domestic crop we turn to apples producers down under
for more.

Of the more than five hundred apple varieties known to
us today, only about a dozen or so ever find their way into our
homes. Some of those are pretty tasteless, including the incor-
rectly named Delicious apple, the absurd standard-bearer by
which other and better apples are judged. We have only ourselves
to blame for the lack of consumer demand for more variety in
our apple habit. Ask any commercial grower what traits they
select for in apples and they will tell you "redness, crispness,
and hardness." The first two because that's what we say we
want in an apple, and the third because they keep longer and
travel better. These criteria leave out a lot of really good apples.
It annoys me that flavor and suitability for pies don't make it
into the top three.

The market allows a few yellow- or green-skinned
apples into the club, but gone forever are those with russeted
skin. Lord's Seedling, Canada Reinette, and Ashmead's Kernel
all have patches of brown skin on them like that of a Bosc pear,
and none of them have a chance in the marketplace because of
it. The Golden Russet is a favorite of mine but I can't get it
very often. There are few apple orchards that grow antique
varieties of apples. Ski-Hi Fruit Farm outside of Baraboo,
Wisconsin, has a few trees of several antique apples and if I

make the trip there at the right time of year and if they have any left, I can get a bag or two of Golden Russets. Like many other apple varieties, the Golden Russet doesn't taste like anything special when first picked; it needs a period of cold storage to coax its glories out. Old-timers with a vast and sophisticated knowledge of these older varieties have taught me not to eat my first Golden Russet until Christmas Day and not before. But it is worth the wait; the Golden Russet has sublime undertones of butter and spice not encountered in other apples.

The Yellow Transparent is another antique variety lost to modernity. It is neither red, nor crisp, nor hard, but it is one of the very first apples of the season. The Yellow Transparent and the Lodi, its offspring, get used for making applesauce because they burst into juice and sloppy pulp when cooked. The apples are soft and quickly grow mealy, so they don't store well. But when picked at just the right moment they make a particularly luscious pie. My grandmother GeeGee used Yellow Transparent for her early pies and I thought they were the best of all, even better than my mother's pies. They were buttery and sweet and reminded me of fresh-mown hay and the first sweet corn.

An old farmer down the road from me has a home orchard with a few interesting antique apples. The Wedge is a variety introduced by the University of Minnesota in the 1920s. It's an easy apple to work with and a good choice for the first-time Pie Maker because it needs no thickening—it melts into just the right consistency for pie. But its flavor, while sweet, lacks distinction. Another variety, the Transmalinda, doesn't lack for anything; it's a wonderful apple for eating or for pie. It's a cross between the Yellow Transparent and the Malinda, an old Russian variety. Most of the apples grown in the North have some Russian in them for hardiness. Duchess and Hibernal are varieties that still grow in the remnants of old orchards in the St. Croix Valley.

I confess that I'm a romantic about antique apple varieties, partly because of the whimsical names. Who wouldn't want to try an apple named Red Butterscotch, Winter Banana, or Chenango Strawberry? Who would not be seduced by Sops of Wine, Pink Pearl, Maiden's Blush, or Summer Rose? Curiosity alone begs us to seek out Hog Sweet, Yellow Sheepnose, Mountain Boomer, and the Westfield Seek-No-Further. And just for the sheer delight of saying the name, I'd like to try Fallawater Pippin, Belle de Boskoop, or Hubbardston's Nonesuch.

Some of these apples possess special qualities of late flowering, disease resistance, pollination, or storage ability. Some have the taste or smell of clove, cinnamon, mint, banana, walnut, raspberry, or cherry. And some, it must be confessed, really aren't that good, given newer varieties. The apple possesses a vast gene pool; these varieties and thousands of others over time and space manifest the range of possibilities. That's why the monoculture of the red, hard, and crisp apples bothers me so. The Delicious apple is a tyrant, a bullying silverback alpha apple hogging all the space in lunch bags, cafeterias, and produce bins. It's like a media conglomerate that homogenizes public taste and dictates choice while restricting the same. I'm sure it was a Delicious apple that banished Adam and Eve, poisoned Snow White, and scared little William Tell half to death.

If it were up to me to choose just one apple that would set the standard for all the rest, I wouldn't choose Delicious. I'd choose McIntosh, with Cortland and Transmalinda as runners-up. These three apples combine a snappy tartness with enough undercurrents of other flavors to add character and depth. The descriptions of lots of apples say they are fine for eating and cooking, but read between the lines; this means they are okay at both, but not excellent. The McIntosh, the Cort, and the Trans provide truly excellent flavor and handling. They have the nostalgia factor going for them too—they are Yankee apples and I'm a Yankee. Two of those four apple trees in my New Jersey backyard were McIntosh.

In Minnesota the Haralson is by far the most popular apple. Apple growers here embraced this new variety developed by the University of Minnesota with native pride. It's a good apple as far as it goes, but it lacks the depth and punch of my beloved Mac. What the Haralson does have going for it is, well, redness, crispness, and hardness. But when it comes to making an apple pie, none of those qualities matter; it's the flavor that counts most. And there's one other quality—does the apple hold a slice? That's Pie Talk for whether an apple mushes up when cooked and the slices are indistinguishable from each other, or if the slices hold their shape.

This is where I disagree with many other discerning Pie Makers and Pie Eaters. Their esteem of an apple pie rises or falls on this one quality alone. I've never understood this fixation on texture. I think it must have something to do with how early solid food was introduced to them as infants. When I go to my favorite orchard to buy apples, the people there practically give away the McIntosh to me because it isn't hard or crisp enough for most. The Mac doesn't hold a slice; never has, never will.

When I've quizzed other Pie Makers on the apple they like to use most for pie, they most frequently mention Haralson, McIntosh, and Northern Spy. I've made a study of all locally grown apples to see which makes the best pie. Macs and Corts are by far my favorites, but I also discovered the virtues of a few others. The Honeygold makes a very sweet, buttery-tasting pie. Oriole provides a little more tartness. The best of the early apples is the Paula Red. From February through July there are a dearth of good North American apples, but the best of the lot are Jonathan.

There are a couple of promising newcomers coming through the pipeline from the fun folks at the Minnesota Horticultural Research Center. A few years ago they let me try out some different apples they were still evaluating before commercial release. I tested about two dozen and most were so-so. But one stood head and shoulders above the rest—the Honeycrisp. Since its release several years ago, the Honeycrisp has become the rock star of Minnesota apples. It's red, it's crisp, it's hard—but it also has great flavor. It may soon outpace the Haralson for the Minnesota palate, but I'm still sticking with my Macs.

The other ingredient that can make or break an apple pie is cinnamon. Some Pie Makers might also add nutmeg, mace, cloves, or star anise, but cinnamon is the dominant spice. The ground bark of the cinnamomum tree or cassia bush marries so perfectly with apples that we cannot imagine apple anything without cinnamon. The French do not share this view; they never put cinnamon or other spices in their apple tarts.

Most people are unaware of the limitations of cinnamon purchased off the shelf in grocery stores. Ground up years ago, exposed to extremes of temperature and sunlight and bad storage conditions, it is at best a shadow of its true nature. I do not make shy pies. Because I want blood and passion in them, I take my cinnamon very seriously. I buy it special each year from Penzeys Spice House and I wouldn't enter the height of pie season without it. Penzeys carries four different cinnamons—from Indonesia, China, Sri Lanka, and Vietnam—and each is wonderful in its own way. My favorite is the 6 percent Extra-Fancy Vietnamese Cassia Cinnamon. This is the dominatrix of all cinnamons. It is rich, intoxicating, sexy, and exotic. This cinnamon wakes you up, slaps you around a little, and makes you gasp. It doesn't have a style—it has an agenda.

The traditional accompaniments for a slice of apple pie are ice cream or a slice of orange cheese. I'm usually not one to gild the lily, but a wedge of New York cheddar with a piece of apple pie makes it a complete food. A baby could grow up just fine if it ate nothing but apple pie and cheese. This is my favorite combination for when I indulge in that wonderful Yankee custom of having pie for breakfast. Better than getting a good horoscope in the morning paper, pie for breakfast sets everything right for the rest of the day. Even if nothing else gets accomplished, it has not been a wasted day.

Apple Dumpling Pie

The "No Excuse for Not Making a Pie" Pie

There are those among you who could enjoy the pleasures of a homemade pie with greater frequency if you could be persuaded to try to make one. This recipe is for you, the timid of soul who frets about pie dough sticking to the rolling pin. It is a forgiving pie—let it embolden you to greater efforts. It is also for you, the busy, accomplished cook, running out of time and about to sacrifice the dessert course in favor of a shower. Let this pie amuse you with its simplicity and rustic style. No less of a pie because it is easy, it will do everything its big brothers and sisters do, and will do it more often.

Crust:

1½ cups flour

½ teaspoon salt

1 tablespoon sugar

½ cup shortening

4 tablespoons ice water

Filling:

½ teaspoon cinnamon

⅓ cup sugar

4 cups apples, peeled, cored, and sliced

1 teaspoon lemon juice

- Preheat the oven to 425 degrees.

- Combine the flour, salt, and sugar in a bowl; cut in the shortening with two knives or a pastry blender until it resembles coarse meal.

- Sprinkle the ice water on 1 tablespoon at a time and toss to mix.

- Gather up the dough into one firm ball and flatten it into a thick disk with your hands.

- Roll out the dough until it is a rough circle about 14 inches in diameter. It should be a little thicker than for a conventional pie.

- Place the crust onto a round pizza pan; do not bother to trim the edges.

- Mix the cinnamon into the ⅓ cup sugar well; reserve 1 teaspoon.

- Sprinkle the sliced apples with the lemon juice and then the cinnamon-sugar mixture.

- Place the apple-sugar mixture onto the center of the piecrust.

- Pull the edges of the piecrust over the apples, flattening the pile of apples somewhat. Don't cover the apples completely; leave a gap of about 4 inches in diameter in the middle.

- Brush the top of the pie with water, milk, or beaten egg and sprinkle with the reserved teaspoon of cinnamon-sugar.

- Bake at 425 degrees for 15 minutes, then turn the oven down to 350 degrees and bake for 25 more minutes.

- Let cool, then cut into six or eight wedges.

9

(• REST STOP •)

MILE 118—THE STING

He has an oar in every man's boat,

and a finger in every pie.

—Miguel de Cervantes Saavedra, from *Don Quixote*

One spring I sent my brother and sister-in-law on a precious errand. Our parents were visiting a sister in the Milwaukee area and John and Susan were going to drive over there from Minneapolis to visit them. I wasn't able to go but I made two rhubarb pies and sent them along with them. They swung by my place to pick them up, then headed east on the interstate. They planned to arrive in the afternoon and the pies were dessert for that night's dinner.

They were practically salivating from the sight and aroma of the two rhubarb pies in the car, but they knew they didn't dare sample them. Instead they stopped for lunch in some small town off the interstate. The pies stayed in the car.

When they returned to their car, they saw that all the fluid that used to be in their radiator wasn't there anymore; it lay in a puddle at their feet. Uh-oh, what were they going to do now? It was a Sunday afternoon and there were no garages open in this little burg of 584 citizens. Two hundred miles away, our parents and sister were awaiting the arrival of the pies with eager anticipation.

"Can I help you?"

They looked up and saw a lanky young man who had passed the boy stage of his development but not yet arrived at the man stage.

"Looks like you got a bad radiator."

He told them of a garage nearby, just up the hill on the way back to the interstate. Sure, it was closed now, it being Sunday and with the ball game on TV, but he knew the guy and called him up. The young man phoned, set the whole thing up for them, then offered to bring their car up there with his tow truck. The garage owner said, "Hi, where you headed?" and talked the highway talk that men do when they need to get to know each other a little bit.

"Might take a couple of hours to get a radiator in."

"Well, we can't go anywhere now anyway."

"That's right, you can't."

"Do you take credit cards?"

"Of course we do. This is Packer country."

The garage owner and the lanky young man with the tow truck got to work. John and Susan walked back into town, strolled around the village green about eight times, walked to the playground and tried out every swing, and on Main Street poked their heads into the antique store, the craft shop, and the Rexall. They phoned ahead to let the anxious relatives know the situation and their new arrival time. They puttered around this town of 584 people for two and a half hours, then walked back up the hill to the garage.

The pies sat in the backseat of the car the entire time. It's a good thing they were not cream or custard pies because the heat in the garage would not have done them any good. It's certain that the garageman and the lanky young tow-truck man observed the pies in the backseat of the car. We can only wonder what they thought about them and any comments that might have passed their lips. We can be sure that the pies caught their attention because you don't see pies like that every day. If the men said anything at all, the pies were the only ones to hear.

The car was done. The pies lay in the backseat just as before. No one knew if they had been moved, sniffed at, or lovingly caressed and admired, but it wouldn't surprise me if they had been. My brother offered up his MasterCard and the garageman rang up the charge. The labor cost was half what it would have been back in Minneapolis. The parts charge was almost negligible, for they had found a radiator in a spare parts yard. If you could pick a place to get a radiator repaired, it should be that place.

The transaction complete, my brother and the garageman exchanged brief pleasantries and more highway talk. Both were taciturn sort of men yet talked more than their usual habit. Something lay unresolved between them. Those pies burned a hole in their consciousness but they couldn't find a way to bring it up. They talked in ridiculous circles about Highway 41 and Highway 43 and the detour in the Dells and the speed traps on the interstate. They got so lost in their talk they didn't know how to get themselves out, so they kept on talking until they had driven themselves from one end of Wisconsin to the other and back again.

All the while my brother wrestled with his conscience. It was just like in first-grade catechism class when the nuns taught us to picture a little red devil with a pitchfork sitting on one shoulder and a white angel with a harp on the other. The devil told him not to bring the subject of the pies up, to just get out of there quickly and take both of the pies with him. Meanwhile the angel exhorted him to be kind and generous, just like the garageman and lanky young man were to him, and offer them one of the pies. Maybe the garageman saw this struggle taking place right before his eyes and all he had to do was keep the conversation going and hope that the angel would win out. Surely he couldn't be that interested in which county road went from West Bend to Cedarburg.

So they talked about roads more until my brother began to sweat bullets. He finally blurted out, "Listen, I've got these two pies. Do you want one?" The garageman and lanky young man smiled at each other. Their plan had worked. They didn't care that they had absurdly discounted their work; they got the prize they wanted. But was it a sting operation? How many other pies had they snared off the highway? Had the lanky young man cased out my brother's car and poked the hole in the radiator himself? I don't know. Maybe that is how they do things in Packer country. ⌁

10

BLUEBERRY

I don't think a really good pie can be made

without a dozen or so children looking

over your shoulder as you stoop to look

in at it every little while.

—John Gould

One year for her birthday, my father bought my mother a movie camera, a Bell and Howell handheld with a set of floodlights for indoor work, and a projector and screen to enjoy the results. They both used it to record reunions, graduations, and the antics of their five children. There was nothing we kids liked better than to hunker down in the living room with bowls of popcorn and watch ourselves as the stars of our home movies. We had favorite scenes that would show each brother and sister in their worst temperament or most embarrassing posture. There are two such scenes for me, one of which I won't tell you about and the other I will. It was an indoor sequence, so my father used the monsterlike apparatus of floodlights that bleached all the color out of faces. I was eight years old, gawky, my hair crimped by a bad home perm, and I wore a purple-and-white dress with big polka dots. My two front teeth were missing and I was eating a piece of blueberry pie.

My father no doubt saw the possibilities in this setup, probably envisioned a rhapsody of purple-and-white cinema verité. He got me to laugh for the camera, kept up the jokes, and zoomed in to preserve my purple mouth for eternity. The parents and sibs trotted this scene out for years to show their friends, my boyfriends, all our relatives, and even a couple of strangers what a freak of nature I was.

Even with this purple mortification, I loved blueberry pie. It was and remains a favorite. Each type of pie has a lesson to impart, and it can take years to learn it. Each has its own personality, history, difficult little habits or postures, but at its core is its one central truth. Rhubarb pie is about Wisdom. Apple pie is about Honor. And blueberry—blueberry pie is about Innocence.

The blueberry is one of the few fruits native to North America. It likes to grow in the sandy and acid understory of pine forests. In its wild state it is a low-growing little bush with fruit the size of pellets. With commercial cultivation it attains shrub proportions with fruit the size of marbles. In New Jersey, where I grew up and served my pie apprenticeship, blueberries were part of the landscape. The Pine Barrens were home to several commercial growers, and at the height of the season, my mother would buy cases of blueberries at 25 cents a pint. There are good reasons why New Jersey is called the Garden State and not the Chemical Manufacturing State—this is one of them. My job was to cull and package this bounty to be placed in frozen reserve for future pies. We made only token gestures to other uses of blueberries—muffins, pancakes, on top of the morning cereal—for in our house, blueberry pie was second only to apple.

I won't say we got bored with apple pie—that never happened—but sometimes we wanted something different, something more playful than the gravitas and work of apple. Berries of any sort can put the fun back into pies. They are the Beaujolais of pies and apple is the Burgundy. And berries are small and don't need to be peeled, pitted, or sliced. You just pour two pints into a pie shell and you are already half done.

As a child, I spent every Fourth of July in East Smithfield,

Pennsylvania, at my grandmother GeeGee's house. The noon parade went right by her place, the hope of a nation on display in floats and flags and high school bands. She and my parents watched from the porch, waving at veterans and beauty queens from behind the wisteria vine. We kids stood or sat on the curb and peppered the sidewalk with exploding cracker balls and caps. The parade dazzled us with its importance, and even though these were all local people and businesses, we thought they must be very significant to be in a parade. One year, Miss Pennsylvania was in the parade, and as her float wafted by, she looked directly at me from her high perch and waved with special significance in her wrist. I felt chosen to receive some special knowledge. The end of the parade was always disappointing because we were children and we wanted more, more, more. What to do with us until dusk, when the fireworks began? Feed us. And a midday dinner of chicken and biscuits, sliced tomatoes, and blueberry pie appeared, and we ate and ate, and then the parents laid their sleepy-headed children down for naps and probably tried to catch one themselves.

The association of blueberry pie with the Fourth of July is so strong for me that I try to re-create this moment of innocence each year and make one for my family, though sometimes the heat of the day gets the better of me and I substitute

cool slices of watermelon instead. I put my Proustian moment
off for later, for July is young and there will be blueberries
all month.

As I traveled and moved about, I either found the blueberries or the blueberries found me. Some special kinship
between blueberries and myself evolved over time. I grew from
child to young adult, learning the ways of the blueberry, both
wild and cultivated. Transplanted from the East to the Midwest,
I spent a summer during college working as a naturalist in a
Minnesota state park and I found my blueberries in the pine
forests of the North Woods. During my time off I took to the
woods with my buckets and picked so many wild blueberries I
had to invent new ways to eat them. After pies, blueberry
malted milks were a favorite that summer. I didn't know all
that much about the natural history of the park, but I knew
where the blueberries were and who my competition for them
was—bears! We avoided each other.

Later on as a married woman, I spent a year in Europe
with my husband. We began our adventure in the late summer
in Sweden and there were still blueberries to pick. I spent many
hours roaming the woods in search of the last blueberries and
lingonberries. If there is a more peaceful and contemplative
pursuit, I don't know what it is. The blueberry (genus *Vaccinium*)
is related to heather (genus *Calluna*) and it was in Sweden that

I saw them together; rocky outcroppings in the woods decorated with tufts of heather and ground-hugging blueberries, their leaves turning bright red alongside the heather's pink and purple.

Eventually I settled down with a house, a family, and a yard and began my pursuit of a home orchard where I would grow all my favorite pie material in abundance. During long winters I pored over garden catalogs, daydreaming of apple trees; which pears would cross-fertilize best; and which cherry cultivar would tolerate subzero temps. There would be raspberries, gooseberries, strawberries, rhubarb, and of course there would be an entire section of the garden devoted to blueberries. Of all the pests that can afflict fruit crops, my dream of a home orchard would never come to pass because of one—deer. But I did not know that at the beginning and I believed I could protect my trees and shrubs with barriers of fences, electricity, fabric, malodorous screens, and hot pepper. The trees succumbed right away to the browsing deer, but the blueberries experienced a long-drawn-out demise that tested the limits of that special kinship.

For my first blueberry investment, I bought six bushes and planted them in an area where I could also enjoy their red color in the fall. It was a foolish mistake, for the deer found them immediately. I put off the inevitable for a couple of years by fashioning coverings that I made out of black nylon net.

They looked like big shower caps. They worked for about two months, but then the branches became horribly entangled in the net as they grew and I ended up having to cut them off. I finally dug the bushes up and moved them to a more protected spot. The deer found that one, too, and in another year I transplanted them again. This time I tried to think like a deer. I wrestled a fence around the new garden, adding height and breadth to it as best I could. I was going to plant everything in here and do whatever it took to keep the deer out. This seemed like a good time to add to my holdings, so I bought fifteen more blueberry bushes. I could practically smell all those blueberry pies and taste their bright sweetness as I laid them out in rows and put down pine needles for their mulch. The next year, my color-blind husband, who has trouble with greens and browns, rototilled a row into near oblivion. Year after year, I mulched, weeded, watered, protected, and got only handfuls for my efforts. Trees began to grow up, shading them, making matters worse. The deer jumped the fence like Olympic gymnasts. Birds came and dropped the seeds of other berries behind and now I can't tell the blueberries from the buckthorn. And the innocence of my Garden of Eden slowly ended, not with the bite of an apple, but with the steady encroachment of a natural cycle I really didn't know enough about.

Blueberries, especially cultivated ones, can have a blandness to them. When I make a blueberry pie I add some lemon zest as well as lemon juice and a generous grating of whole nutmeg. If I have a handful of currants, I add those too for some tartness. Blueberries have a natural affinity to lemon. One Pie Maker I know reverses these proportions and adds a cup of blueberries to the custard of her lemon meringue pie for an amusing polka-dot version of the standard. But the bigger challenge to turning out a great blueberry pie is thickening the juices. Like all berries, blueberries become very juicy when cooked. More than once I've cut a first slice out of a blueberry pie only to have all the fruit swim out in a tide of its own juices. Something must be done about that. The idea is to increase the viscosity of the juice, to reduce its flow to a slow ooze. There is a whole science around thickenings for pie, but here is what I do. For every 4 cups of berries I add 3 tablespoons of cornstarch to the sugar instead of the more usual 2 tablespoons. It helps to mix the cornstarch really well into the sugar, and then to toss the blueberries with the sugar to distribute it throughout the pie.

WHEN CARLA WAS CALLED
TO BLUEBERRY

The proof of a good cook is not in an excellent sauce, a finely roasted joint of meat, or a successful soufflé. No, the proof is whether the cook can accomplish these things while cooking in a trench. Carla Kingstad, my mother-in-law, was such a cook. She earned her title as a Queen of Pies and received her calling on the same occasion of a family vacation in the Canada woods. The Kingstad family (two parents and six kids in that same rhythm pattern that the Dimocks used to great effect) took a vacation in 1962 with the West Allis Rod and Gun Club crowd. For two weeks they camped and fished with the other families of the Rotten Gun Club, as Carla liked to call it. If my mother-in-law had other ideas about the sort of vacation she'd like to take she either kept them to herself or did not prevail, I don't know which, but I believe that two weeks of making camp in Lake of the Woods with six children led her to think of many things. Joined by other members of the Rotten Gun Club, the Kingstads set out as a game band of hunters and gatherers united in the eternal quest for the Big One.

Wild blueberries begin to ripen in mid-July in the Far North. In 1962 this coincided with the birthday on

July 20 of one of the children, the fifth birthday for little David. A birthday cake with frosting and candles was not on the camp kitchen menu. Carla, already predisposed to hearing a calling by virtue of staying in camp with all those children while the men fished, sensed something new was upon her. She rounded up all the children and took to the woods with pails and buckets and returned with gallons, no, oceans of wild blueberries.

What led her to make pies in camp? It's hard enough in a kitchen. Was it the challenge or the chance to show off her skills? Was it lunacy? I did not know her then—I've only heard the stories—but knowing what I do about pies, I believe that she received her call. When Nature bestows the gift of that many wild blueberries, you know that there are greater forces at work, and it becomes a moral obligation to put on the mantle.

So Carla set to work. She rounded up all the deep-dish camp plates. She peeled and smoothed a birch log to use as a rolling pin. She rounded up flour, sugar, and Crisco from the camp pantry. But what to do about some lemon? Blueberry pies had to have some lemon or other tartness. There were no lemons at the campground and none in the cabin store on the other side of the lake. Not even lemonade. Back then, Kool-Aid made a flavor called grapefruit. Who knows what it really was, but it was sour and would have to stand in for lemon. Carla cleared off all available work surfaces and went at it with a zeal that did not end until she turned out twelve pies. It took the entire afternoon to bake them, two at a time, in some makeshift camp oven. I can't imagine how she did it.

Later that evening, with everyone back at camp, the birthday festivities began. In addition to the Rotten Gun Club crowd, Carla invited the entire campground over for dessert. Strangers wandered over with a cup of coffee in one hand and a handshake on the other. The pies were sliced and served all around and everybody said it was the best blueberry pie they'd ever had. And it was the best they ever would have. Everyone joined in singing "Happy Birthday," then gave Carla the standing ovation she deserved. Little David, amazed at the size of his birth-day chorus, simply beamed. The campground was awash with goodwill, full bellies, and new friends from this modern-day camp miracle of loaves and fishes.

Carla's North Woods blueberry pies gained her automatic entry into that rarefied strata of Pie Makers—the Queens of Pie. In the eyes of her family she was already a Queen and would remain so forever, but this occasion announced to the world that a new Queen walked among them, and they would recognize her by the purple stains on her fingertips.

A hungry fork sweeps up the stray crumbs and a napkin dabs at dribbles of juice. The purple stains of blueberries are gentle artifacts of youth and nostalgia. Bright splotches now, they will be a faint gray by this time next year. The tablecloth carries the stories of an eight-year-old girl in a polka-dot dress and a mother of six who went into the woods and found oceans of blueberries. Flags and parades, fireworks and friends, bear and deer—they've all worked their way into the fabric.

Carla's North Woods Blueberry Pie

6 children

A campground of strangers

No radio

A log

3 packets grapefruit Kool-Aid

Flour, sugar, shortening, salt

A rocky island in the middle of a lake with lots of pine trees

12 deep-dish camp plates

A sunny day

- Send the children out into the woods to find the blueberries.

- Use a hatchet to remove the bark and any knobs from a log to use as a rolling pin.

- Make the dough for the crust and form it into twenty-four balls.

- Roll out twelve of them, using the log, and place them in the camp plates.

- Fill the plates with as many blueberries as they will hold.

- Sprinkle ½ cup sugar, 2 tablespoons flour, and ¼ packet grapefruit Kool-Aid onto each pie.

- Roll out the other twelve balls of dough with the log, place them on the pies, and trim and seal them.

- Bake the pies. (Oh, right—we're on an island in the middle of a lake in the North Woods.)

- Make a reflector oven—somehow. Maybe one of those children is a Girl or Boy Scout.

- Bake the pies.

- Sing songs until the pies are done. (No radio, remember?)

- Invite all the campground strangers over for a piece of pie.

- Everybody introduces themselves.

- Put these people on your holiday greeting card list.

- Remember this day for the rest of your life.

11

Thanksgiving Pie

Ah! on Thanksgiving day, when from East
and from West,
From North and from South, come the pilgrim
and guest,
When the gray-haired New Englander sees
round his board
The old broken links of affection restored,
When the care-wearied man seeks his mother
once more,
And the worn matron smiles where the girl
smiled before.
What moistens the lip and what brightens the eye?
What calls back the past, like the rich
Pumpkin pie?

—John Greenleaf Whittier

CHAIN LETTER AND RECIPE

Dear Friend,

You have been selected to receive this chain letter because of something you did somewhere, sometime, for someone. This act of yours mattered and was remembered with gratitude by the sender of this letter. So for a moment, sit back and delight in the surprise of being remembered for your good works. You deserve it.

This chain letter began in Afton, Minnesota, in November 1993 to celebrate and make personal the spirit and intent of Thanksgiving Day. The chain is no longer confined to November, nor to that little corner of the world where it started. Gratitude knows neither season nor boundaries.

This is not your ordinary chain letter. This chain letter will not bring you good luck. It will not make you rich, nor prevent you from cruel misfortune. You won't get anything back from this chain letter. It's not about getting, it's about giving—Thanksgiving.

Unlike other chain letters, you do not have to send books, money, stamps, aprons, cards, or dish towels to a name at the top of a list. You do not have to respond within seven days or risk a lifetime of bad luck and misfortune. You do not have to weigh guilt or annoyance before hitting the delete key. You do not have to do anything at all; the chain can go on without you. But if you choose to join in, you will cause hundreds more to be thanked for something good they did in their lives. You will sleep better tonight and a friend just might cross the street to hug you rather than only wave. You will have the great enjoyment of knowing that you are part of life's fabric and have been both weaver and tailor.

The pie recipe is to share because pies are an important way of saying thank you. Like compliments and recognition, there are never enough good pies, and this one has all the wonder and delight of the discovery of a new star. It is not a difficult pie to make. Even if you are only halfway competent in the kitchen, you should be able to pull it off just fine. Try to make this pie and deliver it along with your letter. This recipe was created as part of a traditional Thanksgiving feast, no matter where or when it is celebrated.

To keep the chain going, just copy and send this letter by e-mail, snail mail, or hand delivery. There is no list of names to cross off or add to, but there is a space at the bottom to write your own personal thank you. Be specific about your appreciation. Send it to no fewer than two people, for surely there are at least two people you are beholden to for something. Start your own branch and see it wind through your family, childhood friendships, teammates, work partners, teachers and coaches, former bosses, even people whose names you don't know. Do it now while that reckless impulse is still fresh in you. You will never regret it. And you don't have to stop at two. You don't have to stop at all.

If the chain is never broken, it may go around the world three times and be translated into fourteen languages, but more important, the simple act of giving thanks will assume a life of its own. And sometime when least expected, you might receive the letter again, thanking you for a kindness you thought long forgotten. What goes around, comes around. As it should.

With kind regards,

[your name here]

Thanksgiving Pie

Crust:

1 (9- or 10-inch) piecrust, prepared or made from scratch. My crust recipe is on page 111.

Filling:

3 apples (use a soft, sweet variety like McIntosh or other sauce variety)
1 (12-ounce) package fresh whole cranberries
1 cup light brown sugar

Topping:

¾ cup walnuts
¼ cup light brown sugar
¼ cup white flour
3 tablespoons butter, softened or cut into bits
½ teaspoon cinnamon
⅛ teaspoon salt

- Preheat the oven to 425 degrees.

- Prepare the piecrust and fit into a 9- or 10-inch pie pan.

- Peel, core, and dice the apples.

- Place the apple pieces in a large bowl with the cranberries and 1 cup of light brown sugar; mix well and place into the pie shell.

- Place the walnuts in the bowl of a food processor fitted with the steel blade; pulse for 5 seconds.

- Add the remaining ingredients and pulse until blended but still crumbly. (If you don't have a food processor, chop the nuts by hand and blend them with the rest of the ingredients with the back of a large spoon.)

- Spoon the topping all over the pie.

- Bake at 425 degrees for 20 minutes, then lower the temperature to 350 degrees for 30 more minutes; cover with foil to prevent the topping from darkening too much.

12

◉ REST STOP ◉

MILE 189—
SOMEWHERE IN WISCONSIN

God's always got a custard pie

up his sleeve.

—Margaret Forster

I was hopeful about this next place. A cute little town on a
state highway, it looked tidy and prosperous, as if civic pride
and a community ethos still beat within its public heart. I
walked into the Town Crier Bakery and Café and evaluated the
pie display case. Blueberry, peach, cherry, and apple. I had my
doubts—the ooze factor looked way too high on all of them
except the peach. Only the peach showed a slow gush of fruit

juice, so I ordered a slice in spite of the fact that ripe peaches were more rare in this part of the country than zebras.

It was the most disappointing pie I've ever had. The peaches were pure Libby's canned slices and the pale ooze that tricked me was heavy syrup from the can supersaturated with sugar and cornstarch. I could even taste the tin can. It was the sort of pie I've always wondered about. Why would anyone go to the trouble of making a homemade crust and then put that stuff in it? I left most of it on the plate and bought a toothbrush on my way out of town. ∾

13

PIE AS FEMINIST TOOL

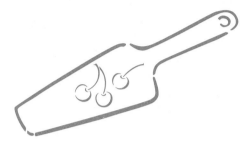

What [else] is pie for?

—Ralph Waldo Emerson, when questioned about
the New England habit of eating pie for breakfast

Pies always conjure up an image of wholesome women. Once it was Betty Crocker in a gingham apron. Now it is the good-looking young mothers in lifestyle catalogs, with children and home trendily attired, and a token man struggling with his crust. (Don't the men always struggle with their crust?) Mom and apple pie will always be part of our national mythology, as well as the Thanksgiving Day tableau of five pies cooling on the sill, Grandma wiping her brow but still smiling.

No matter how this scene is updated, we will always

carry around the cultural baggage of Women-Who-Know-How-to-Make-Pies and Men-Who-Know-How-to-Eat-Them. The images are clear—making pies is women's work and men's relish.

Then there is the side you don't see. We don't want you to—it's our little secret. There's a lot more going on with the women making most of the world's pies than domestic harmony or saintly acts of sacrifice. There's power. It's the same power exercised by any group that must live with another group more numerous or powerful. It's a power that comes from quiet observation and deep knowledge about your competition. It is very useful to know everything about people who hold power over you, and pie is an important tool for revealing the truth about the person eating it.

Whenever I wanted a particular man to start paying attention to me, I would start making pies. A simple and obvious flirtation? No. I didn't make the pies to attract the man; I made the pies to test him. Any man can follow his nose and track the scent of a homemade pie. What good is that? All it gets you is a man who wants another pie. How do you know if he is the kind of man worth making another pie for? That's the kind of knowledge that's worth the price of learning how to make pies.

Some men regard pie as an entitlement, requiring a weekly or even daily fix. At their worst, these men are selfish and will take your pie, and you, for granted. But at their best, these men know pie and they know why yours is better than anybody else's and why only yours will do. They know that pie is important in their lives, but they don't know why. Don't waste any scorn on them; they are to be pitied. These are also the men unlikely to stray, though you may wish to lose them once in a while.

Other men will be fixated on one type of pie. They are the ones who pout when their pie isn't in the usual five-pie Thanksgiving Day lineup. They are the reason why five different pies are served. Disappointed when their favorite pie isn't included, they drive their mothers into pie baking frenzies, for they equate pie only with how much they are loved. These guys are immature, and you want to shake them and say "Grow up!" Don't bother. Next time they insist on their favorite pie, give it to them—right in the face.

You can tell even more about a man from his reactions to a piece of pie. You don't need me to tell you what to stay away from—the ones who don't say anything, the ones who don't chew, the ones who ask for a second slice before thanking you for the first, the ones who use a spoon. You already know what you're in for with them. But subtle gestures like the place-ment of his arms when he's done or the drop of his chin can speak volumes about a man's nature. The next time you need to evaluate the character of a man, prepare the pie of your choice, give him an ample slice, and yourself a smaller one. This is not a sacrifice, it's strategy. Let him eat, let him talk—you watch.

Pie is a window to a man's soul, a lens by which you can see his true nature and know the measure of his worth. You won't be able to take it all in, not in one slice of pie, not in a thousand. Pie is so revealing—especially rhubarb pie. But to start with, you can choose several traits and look to confirm their presence.

- Is he generous of nature? Look at how he cuts the pie. How large are the bites? Not very? Good.

- Does he bear down on his fork with his index finger? He should.

- Does he take a bit of crust with each bite or leave it to the last? Oh, the last!

- Be mindful of where he begins to eat the slice. While most of us will start at the apex, a particularly curious and lively soul will start elsewhere.

- Watch for pauses. Count them. As the number increases, so does his attention to the details of life.

- Digging out the filling reveals a propensity to lie.

- Nibbling away at the rest of the pie in the pan predicts a man who wants to have things both ways.

- And oddly enough, slow, thoughtful chewing has no relation to introspection, but only to how acute his sense of smell is.

These are the basics. In time you will get to know others. The advantages in courtship are obvious, but don't overlook its applications to the power lunch, the job interview, and the faculty meeting.

What pie reveals is how well a man can identify his hunger. How large and looming is that hunger? Can he name it? How does he meet it? How does he greet it? In the feast of life, will he save room for the pie?

These are very good things to know about men. ∽

14
ZEN AND THE ART OF MAKING PIECRUST

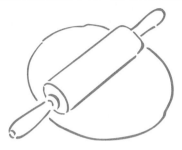

Life is a pie which you cut in large slices, not grudgingly, not sparingly.

—Alice Foote MacDougall

Making piecrust is the art and chemistry of combining separate things into a whole that is greater than the sum of its parts. It is knowledge of the physical world matched with mastery of one's own temperament.

My grandmother GeeGee always said, "You don't want to make your crust too short." That term "short" confused me for the longest time. I took it literally and thought she meant to be sure to roll it out large enough. No, that wasn't what she meant.

She meant don't put too much shortening in——"shortening" as in shortcake, shortening bread, or shortening biscuits. Lard, goose grease, schmaltz, butter, oleo, or Crisco. She was from the "butter the size of a walnut" school of cooking, recipes based upon comparisons rather than standards. I came to rely upon a tried-and-true formula, the three-to-one ratio of flour to shortening with a dash of salt and a jot of sugar.

Grandmother GeeGee also said, "You don't want to work your crust too much." But that didn't tell me how long I was to cut, blend, or mix. "Your crust will get too tough." How? And when did I encounter that critical moment when my crust dough would turn from a ripe sheet of gluten and starch ready to burst into flakes, into a sodden piece of shoe leather? "You just know."

Dear Readers, I understand your anxiety. Your first approach to making piecrust does not need to be fraught with this much ambiguity. But alas, it is an art as much as a science and no set of directions will ever be as complete as the one you make up for yourself. Take mine. It starts with "On a dry day . . ."

*On a dry day, decide if you are to be engaged. If so,
then prepare to sweep away the little anxieties of the little parts
of your life. In piemaking, it is best to* think big *and* live big.
*That will get you in the right frame of mind, something just as
important as having the correct crust ratio. Proceed.*

*You will find that the simple fork is an invaluable tool
for making piecrust. Stir the flour in its canister with a fork to
leaven it with air. Make it billowy and light. After you have
increased its volume, dip into it with your measure and level it
with a bit of rhythmic shaking. Gather all you need in this
manner. With the same fork, stir in very well the salt and sugar.
Go get a cup of cool water and have a nice long sip of it. Plunk
a few ice cubes into it and let it sit. If you have magic words,
say them now. If you haven't any, take another sip of water.*

*Measure your shortening and then add an additional
nugget about the size of a quarter, one for each piecrust. Begin
to work this in with the goal of binding the flour to the shortening incompletely. Many books describe this as a cutting
motion—"cut the shortening into the flour until it resembles
coarse cornmeal." Your choice of tools carries some importance
but not so much as a trained eye. You may use two sharp
knives, a pastry cutter, that simple fork, or even your fingers—
they all do what is asked of them with different economies of
effort. Then stop before you think you are done. Stop when the*

sheen of the fat disappears into ripples and folds and bumps and lumps and specks and flakes. Stop when you no longer discern the white from the not-quite-white. Stop and go no further.

The coolness of the ice water will stay any fever to overwork this amalgam—take another sip. Water, the essential element of so many transformations, will change this dry mass into a smooth, soft dough. Baptize the mixture, sprinkle over the water a tablespoon at a time, and with a deft and light hand use that noble fork to lift and toss, to dance that dough around in its bowl—no body-crashing polka but a lilting mazurka— that will do it!

Here you must make a choice, one that will seal the fate of your piecrust for good or for ill. You must draw upon all sensory perception, those of touch, of sight, but especially those that slumber within and waken with memory and experience. Gather up the almost-dough with your hands and decide if it is to drink more water. Watch how it falls apart, whether a squeeze rents it in two or leaves an impression of your hand. The careless are unobservant and will not read the signs of an overly dry dough. They will be tormented with a crust that shatters at their touch. The timorous add more water just to be safe. Their dough will be slightly sticky, and the baked crust pallid and lacking in flavor. You must look hard and then close your eyes and aim for the path between

these two. One teaspoon, maybe two. You will be rewarded
with greatness.

   It is best to take a moment here to prepare yourself for
the next step. Reflect upon what has brought you to this place,
to this moment, to the task set before you. What intentions
have you brought with you? Music can be a great help. Listen
to something with the melancholy aloneness of true genius—
Mozart, Villa-Lobos, Britten. When the music has filled you and
has nowhere else to go but out through your fingers, proceed.

   Gather the dough into two slightly unequal balls, then
flatten the larger one into a round disk. (The Verrazano-
Narrows suspension bridge had to take the curvature of the
Earth into account when calculating its length. Your bottom
crust will need to be slightly larger than your top crust to
accommodate the extra surface area of the pie dish. Same
principle.) Pack the edges together with the side of your hand.
Don't think about how to do this, just let the motion roll forth
from your hands. Dust both surfaces with flour and commence
to roll. Start from the center and roll outward. With each roll,
return to the center and go out again in another direction. (You
may read much about how this is to equalize the tension running
throughout the crust. I've considered this. Are there fault lines
where two plates of crust meet and begin to become part of
one another? When a crust shudders and breaks apart along

an unpredicted path, is it because of unequalized tension in the crust or in the person rolling it out?)

If you have come this far without mishap, then you will instinctively know how much further to go. But many of you will be back at the counter wondering how to unstick your dough from the surface. This is when anxiety steps in, when the twin snakes of short temper and lack of confidence wind their way around you and through you to bring your pie making to its knees. Realize you are being tested. Understand that there is more than one way through this. Know, too, that many have passed this way before you and faltered here at the Gates of Enlightenment.

You may have been tempted by the siren song of kitchen gadgets and baking charms. In your apprehension you may have bought rolling pin garments, crust defibrillators, and pastry doo-dahs in the futile hope of avoiding this moment of truth. Alas, they will do you little good; they are not a substitute for technique. Eschew all accoutrements that have not withstood the test of time in your own kitchen. Don't despair—you are allowed your tools. Reach into that kitchen drawer, the one that goes by various names like "the gadget drawer" or "the junk drawer," and pull out the longest and thinnest utensil in there. It could be a spatula, a long knife, bamboo skewers, or a squeegee. If you have magic words, say them now, and quickly work the edge of your implement between your crust and the surface it lays on. Quickly, like a hummingbird sipping water. Lightly, like butterflies mating. In one swift whoosh, run the edge of your tool through the air between the crust and the surface.

If you falter, it may help you first to imagine this as an out-of-body experience. Imagine and really see yourself hovering about the ceiling of your kitchen, looking down upon the pie-making scene. See yourself as a kitchen samurai with a fleet blade held sideways. See yourself as your great-grandmother, a veteran of hundreds of piecrusts. See yourself confidently coaxing the dough from its sticking point with little more than a feather. See yourself as such and then do it.

Extra flour is very useful. Toss some around—underneath, on top, over your left shoulder—but not too much, just a dusting. Commence rolling again and roll out the dough until it is no larger than it should be and no thicker than it wants to be. Stop and perform the samurai trick whenever you feel the dough tugging at you, resisting its fate. It may help to rotate the crust a quarter turn or so, just to get a new perspective on it. When its diameter is an inch or two larger than that of the pie pan, when it is no thicker than glass, when all rents and tears have been patched, you may put the rolling pin down.

Now you confront a different sort of problem—how to

get the crust lying prone on your counter to drape itself into your pie pan. Levitation is a good response but not practical for most of us. You may derive some comfort from knowing that others have contemplated similar problems of raising delicate things into the air and dropping them safely where they are supposed to go and succeeded: Orville and Wilbur Wright. NASA engineers. Flocks of migrating birds. It's been done before and you will do it, too. Try this:

     Take the rolling pin and lay it softly upon the crust about a third of the way from one of the edges. Lift the edge of the crust and wrap it over the rolling pin. Roll the crust onto the pin, but not all the way, leaving about a quarter of it free. Now pick up the rolling pin and move it over the pie plate. Lower it to the plate and position the free edge over the edge of the plate so that there is about ½ inch of overhang. As you unroll the crust from the rolling pin, it will drape itself into the pie plate and be appropriately centered, more or less. It's best not to think too much about this sequence of events. A little tug or tweak will put everything into its right place. Repeat all of this with the other ball of dough after the filling has been added.

This is as far as I can take you, and in truth, you have come a very long way. The path you take to the perfect piecrust is very likely to be different from mine, but if you remember that it is a meditation as well as an object of desire, you'll be fine. And when you arrive and taste the joy you've created with a homemade pie, beautiful crust and all, you will at last understand why it is that the Buddha is always smiling.

Pie Chart for Piecrust

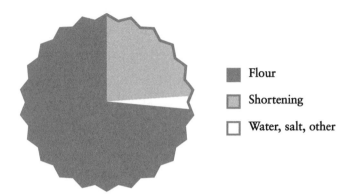

Flour

Shortening

Water, salt, other

Ratios compare one amount to another. A Golden Ratio represents an ideal proportion—indeed, Leonardo da Vinci called it "the divine proportion." Some of the most exquisite art and elegant math in the world is based upon it: Palladian architecture. The Piazza San Marco. Fibonacci numbers. Pascal's Triangle. The spirals of a nautilus shell.

There is a Golden Ratio for piecrust, too. The ratio of 3 to 1, three parts flour to one part shortening, is the divine proportion that all excellent piecrust is based on. Different recipes for piecrust may tweak this just a bit or add some fillip that offers another flavor or texture. Choices abound in types of flour, shortening or other fat, and recipes—enough choices to confuse and intimidate. It is all much simpler than that, as simple as a 3-to-1 ratio. Here is what I use:

1-Crust Pie	2-Crust Pie	Extra-Large 2-Crust Pie
⅓ cup vegetable shortening	⅔ cup vegetable shortening	1 cup vegetable shortening
1 cup all-purpose flour	2 cups all-purpose flour	3 cups all-purpose flour
3 tablespoons ice water	6 tablespoons ice water	9 tablespoons ice water
¼ teaspoon salt	½ teaspoon salt	¾ teaspoon salt
1 teaspoon sugar	2 teaspoon sugar	3 teaspoons sugar

A quick look at this table reveals the simple relationships of the ingredients to one another. As long as the 3-to-1 ratio is followed, you could expand or contract this table to accommodate any number and size of pies. Pie pans usually come in 8-, 9-, or 10-inch diameters. You may occasionally come across pans that are 11 or 12 inches.

The amounts listed here are very forgiving. This will accommodate all manner of errors common to the novice Pie Maker—torn crusts in need of patching, a square crust for a round pan, overly extravagant crimping, a crust too thick or too thin. With experience and confidence comes the skill to stretch the pie dough of a one-crust pie into two, or two crusts into three or four. I can usually eke out double the number of crusts that a beginner can with the same amount of dough, but only experience can lead you to this type of economy. One must never forget the Pie Maker code of generosity and skimp on the crust. After all, the crust is what makes a pie a pie and not stewed fruit. While a thin top crust shows skill, it can also reveal stinginess or make the Pie Maker seem a little too "show-offy." Too thick a top or bottom crust detracts from the experience of the filling. You want a good balance—not unlike the Golden Ratio of 3 to 1.

To make the piecrust, you combine the ingredients and roll out the dough as described in the Zen meditation. When you are finished, you are likely to have some dough left over. Piecrust dough should have a notice on it that says "For One-Time Use Only." The leftovers should not be recycled into another crust. I admit I've done it once or twice, but it's considered bad form and the results usually aren't worth whatever time you've saved. Instead, use the leftover scraps of dough to make Pinwheels, those lovely little grace notes at the end of a pie concerto. My mother and grandmother always used their dough scraps this way, and as children, my siblings and I fought over every one. An *amuse-bouche* of the first order, these little palate teasers forecast the glories to come.

Recipe for Pinwheels

Gather up all the leftover piecrust scraps of dough and wad them into a ball, adding a couple of drops of cold water as the dough is probably drier now. Flatten the ball with your hand and roll it out into a rough rectangle. Moisten the perimeter with a little cold water and sprinkle the entire area with cinnamon-sugar. Roll the dough up tightly lengthwise into a long cylinder, like a jelly roll. Pinch the seam closed. Slice it into rondelles about ½ to 1 inch wide and place them on a cookie sheet. Bake in a preheated 350 degree oven for about 15 minutes until they color to a soft tan.

15

• REST STOP •

MILE 246 —
SOMEWHERE IN MINNESOTA

With the lesson of the last pie stop still fresh in my mind, I decided to test a new variable. Instead of a prosperous-looking little town bisected by state highways, I chose a town that looked like it was going nowhere in the middle of a lonely plain. This place had three diners and I chose the one in the middle, the Cozy Cup. I ordered a slice of apple pie, and while I waited, I reflected upon the cherry pie metaphor in David Lynch's *Twin Peaks*. He was really on to something with the recurring image of cherry pie and coffee, but he didn't take it far enough. Before I was through imagining a couple of alternate endings that had Laura Palmer, Bob, and the dancing midget finding redemption through a piece of pie, my reverie was interrupted by the arrival of my own slice. The waitress placed a cold slab of standard-issue, commercially made apple pie before me. I stared at it for a while, trying to decide if I should eat it. It looked like it had been made by machines and packaged by people wearing hairnets and latex gloves. I nudged it with the fork a little and finally did take a bite. A lot of bad thoughts went through my mind, but I managed to leave the diner without committing any crimes. While driving out of town, I remembered that in *Twin Peaks*, when the diner ran out of pie, the town was plunged into darkness and someone always got hurt. I drove a little faster. ∿

16
THE PRIDE AND THE GLORY

What drives a woman to bake? Sometimes it's a vague, unnamed longing that drives me into the kitchen, a need to work with my hands and create something beautiful and immediate. So much of our work these days is cerebral, done in teams with goals, and months or years away from seeing an effect. Baking is immediate gratification of the first order. The need to establish a connection with others is implicit in baking—a connection to ancestral homeland and people, a beckoning to share, an offer of nourishment. Baking satisfies all sorts of hungers.

But what drives a woman to bake for an audience? To hold herself up, for it is truly her self, to the critical eye of judges who will pick and poke and dissect and taste and scrutinize and decide scores on lots of little things? To go beyond hearth and home and go public?

I had no answer to these questions, nor to my own urge to enter a pie in the Minnesota State Fair. I went to the state fair to find out.

The Minnesota State Fair takes place at the end of August and beginning of September—perfect timing for Pie Makers who've labored hard on their craft all summer. The Monday before the state fair opens is the day when all the hopeful bakers, mostly women but a few men, deliver their entries into the hands of judges who will confer ribbons, honors, and titles. The competition included all types of baked goods—cakes, breads, cookies, and, of course, pies—all subdivided into categories by type, flavor, or ingredients. I went to the drop-off point with my one hopeful entry—a cherry pie—to understand this need for judgment. And to check out the competition.

It's important to understand the preparations leading up to this moment. The days before Competition Monday were a time of intense preparation in the households of state fair competitors. Months of testing and sampling and adjusting came to their conclusion in a weekend marathon of baking. There were a few more trips to grocery stores and farmers' markets to get the freshest whatever that they needed. The rock-hard peaches bought a week ago reached their most ripe loveliness now. The cherries picked and pitted last month with this moment in mind were released from the freezer. The new apples, kept from thieving children, came out of hiding. All was ready to begin.

But this year, the humidity moved in on Saturday and the temperatures shot up on Sunday. Did I mention that this was August in Minnesota, when the weather can rival Bangkok's? The wind stirred up something in the Gulf of Mexico and moved it up the Mississippi Valley. Moisture, the scourge of the baker and Pie Maker, was everywhere and no household was spared. It seeped into every kitchen, every canister and pantry. Like a pestilence, it reached every neighborhood and county. Not even the blood of a lamb on the front door would keep it out. Even those with air-conditioning were not immune, for they would have to leave their homes eventually.

Between the house and the car and the car and the state fair buildings was all it took. What had been crisp and dry became damp in an instant. There would be no pie with a score of a hundred points this year; the humidity took care of that. In one bump of the Gulf Stream, four points disappeared from each pie's score. The flakiness and dryness scores suffered that cruel though not infrequent blow known to Pie Makers as the August Lament. Chaos theory might explain this as the result of the beating of the wings of a butterfly in Singapore that set the fates in motion that would cause the pies in Minnesota to seep, the meringues to weep, the cakes to fall, the icings to run, and the cookies to blur together on their pan. A misfortune for all, but one equally shared.

Competition Monday dawned warm and moist. The bakers and Pie Makers began to arrive with their entries, some having had but an hour or two of sleep. They had been up all night baking, trying to eke out one more point for freshness. They came from near and far. More than one pie arrived warm. Everyone talked about the weather, reciting the Minnesota Mantra, "It's not so much the heat as the humidity," as if that would work some magic and dry things out. It was eight-thirty in the morning and everybody was sweating as they made trips back and forth from their cars to the Creative Activities building.

I noticed that the main competition drove here in vans with custom shelving. Those bakers enlisted husbands and neighbors to help them unload everything. They brought forth pie after pie, cake after cake, just like sixteen clowns leaping out of a Volkswagen Bug. The entries came and came, a parade of pies and cakes and breads and cookies. The most driven competitors brought at least two of everything, and sometimes six. I saw one lady with fourteen of the most luscious-looking cakes I had ever seen—and that was in addition to breads, pickles, jams, and a couple of pies. Most of the entrants were crossover bakers, bringing an entry or two in several different categories. But you could pick out the Pie Makers among them, for they walked like Queens and the crowd parted to let them through.

The bakers brought their entries in boxes, on trays, in laundry baskets, milk crates, and even baby strollers. They wove in and out, stood in line, and juggled plates and trays with children in tow. And maybe even more amazing than this embarrassment of riches was that nobody dropped anything. Just when you thought that had to be it, that there couldn't possibly be more, a round-bellied husband came panting up the sidewalk with two more of his wife's gorgeous pies, his face aglow with pride at bearing such riches, at being the spouse of such a wizard.

This was a level of intensity I was unprepared for. This show of stamina and creative resolve humbled me with my one little cherry pie. Clearly the stakes were higher than I had thought. What drove these women to bake to such heights?

I asked Colleen, a Pie Maker who arrived with four pies, why she came today. She told me that she'd been making pies for over thirty years. She had a large family, seven children, and each one liked a different type of pie. She made about three or four pies every month for her family and another three or four each year for the neighborhood block party. It was her neighbors who suggested she enter them in the fair because the pies were so good. This is the fourth year she had entered some pies at the fair and she had won some sort of ribbon each year. I asked Colleen what was her favorite pie. Without missing a beat, she answered, "Apple."

I asked another Pie Maker, a young woman in her early twenties with beautiful long hair wound up in a French braid, why she had come today. She showed me her cherry pie. This was the first time she had entered the fair although she had been making pies for about eight years. She found that making pies was a good antidote to the grind and routine of daily life. She took the morning off from work to bring the pie in and looked serenely content just standing in line. She had modest hopes for a ribbon, but that had little to do with her decision to enter her pie. She enjoyed the making of the pie for its own sake—that, and having the morning to herself.

I asked Lenora, a veteran of more than twenty-five years of state fair pie contests, why she kept coming back. "It's a hobby," she said. Then she reconsidered her motives. "No, it's more than that. It's like another life." Whether this meant a brand-new life or another chance at the life you already had, I did not know, but either way promised some interesting new territory to explore. Pies could be hints at unlived lives or windows into the richness of experience.

Dorothy came to the fair on a more melancholy mission.

At age seventy-one, she was entering a pie at the state fair for the first time. A husband with Alzheimer's disease had limited her life more completely than she had ever thought possible. It was no surprise to me that her two pies looked divine, for pies are the exquisite expression of a contained life. Dorothy told me that her husband had always been a very skinny man and would eat pie for breakfast. She used to make a couple of pies every week, easily over a hundred every year. But no more. Just a few now and then, for dinner parties, for friends, but not for her husband anymore who found it too confusing to eat anything. "It was good to make a couple of pies again," Dorothy said. "And it's good to get out of the house, too. Everybody always said I made the best pies, so now I'm going to find out if it's true." I could tell by looking at her pies that they would be winners anywhere.

And there was Violet, who had left her recipes at home and now breathlessly jotted them down from memory with only minutes to go before the judging commenced. Yes, she said, this was the first pie she had entered in the state fair. Last year she entered a carrot cake and walked away with the blue ribbon for it. "Now I'm hooked," Violet explained. "I like entering the contests and winning more than I like the actual baking."

I asked each Pie Maker what was their own personal favorite pie. Without exception, they answered apple. A poll of their preferred apple variety for making pies revealed a narrow field—Haralson, Prairie Spy, and McIntosh.

And I asked each Pie Maker why they baked pies for a contest. There wasn't much money involved for prizes, only a paltry $12 for a blue ribbon and it went down from there. "I like the challenge." "I like contests and winning things." "I was bored and needed something to do." "I thought it might be fun." There had to be something else, I thought.

And then I met Trudy, a flamboyant sixty-year-old grandmother in a white miniskirt, with fabulous-looking tanned legs and long "blond" hair. Trudy said she entered things at the fair because it energized her so. She looked positively on fire as she and a neighbor brought in fourteen entries. She looked like she wouldn't need any sleep for a week. Trudy explained that she used to be a vegetarian and a health freak about everything—"Air, water, everything!" Then she was in a car accident two years ago and was laid up for a while in excruciating boredom. Now she's into prime rib and pies and in the throes of a very exciting, vital middle age. "I love making pies. It's fun. It's the creativity I love." One of her pies was beautifully decorated with an Art Deco mosaic of crust circles. Another with an impressionistic rendering of a cherry tree in full bloom. Her neighbor told me that Trudy was also an artist—watercolors—a fantastic gardener, and had been baking pies all her life. I like to think that Trudy, in her free-spirited lust for living, came closest to describing a motivation common to all Pie Makers. "It's absolutely electrifying!"

And that's why the pies came to the state fair, these pies that are like a river, that carry the silt of everyday life with them and deposit it in a rich delta at the judges' table. How would the judges choose? How would they discern the noble distinctions among them? But choose they did, if not with Solomon-like wisdom, then at least with an eye for what would look good on a food magazine cover.

And the winner is—the envelope, please!—Violet! (Beginner's luck again?)

A friendly spirit of competition prevailed. No one went away disappointed. Pie Makers were proud of their own personal best and happy for the success of others. And glad for the recognition too, for this public forum that honored their art with colored ribbons and small checks. While the winners walked away with the prizes, the others could hardly be called losers. Let's call them all "First Runners-up."

Everyone returned home exhausted, but already they had begun planning for next year. Maybe a little less cornstarch. Maybe more butter in the crust. Maybe try a hotter oven. A fine consolation awaited them—the "practice pies," the ones they did not bring today because of their cracked crusts or too much overflow. They were waiting at home like old friends.

And the Minnesota State Fair opened and thousands filed by the display case in the Creative Activities building. There they were, all glistening red and tan. The silent wishes, the pride and the glory that found their expression in pie. ᪰

17

WITH THIS PIE, I THEE WED

I love you as New Englanders love pie!

—Donald Robert Perry Marquis, *Sonnets to a Red-Haired Lady*

The dawn of 1990 was a time unlike any other; great, unexpected events unfolded all around the world.

The Soviet Union was a union no more. Eastern bloc countries declared their independence. The Berlin Wall came down. And on the eve before Nelson Mandela was released from twenty-six years in prison, I got a phone call from my friend Spike. She was in love. The Cold War really was over.

Spike has been my friend for twenty-four years. Patricia is the name she was born with, but Spike is the name she gave herself. Librarians around the world owe Spike a debt of gratitude, for she is one of them and has done more than anyone else to blow away the stereotypes of their profession.

Spike and I make an odd couple of sorts. I won't go so far as to say we are opposites, but the more extreme ends of our personalities balance each other out. One of the things that makes our friendship work is that we are both pie people from way back. With the Pie Makers we had in our respective lineages, we could have been cousins. Whenever we talk about men, we somehow get around to talking about pies. In fact, it was Spike and I who first parsed out the mute language men speak when they eat a piece of pie. Spike knows better than anyone that pies are a powerful tool in courtship. I've seen her through several romances and I can always tell how things are going by the type of pies she bakes. Apple if she is getting interested. Pumpkin, just being polite. Rhubarb for reconciliation, and her favorites, gooseberry or grape, if life is beautiful.

But back to early 1990. I had just seen Spike two weeks earlier when she stopped for the night at my place on one of her many trips from Madison to Minneapolis. We stayed up late talking, laughing, and reminiscing. I had a copy of the book *The Cake Bible* around and we pored over it, looking at all the photographs of beautiful cakes created by Rose Levy Beranbaum. We talked about cakes and pies the way some men talk about sports. I favored anything that had fruit in it, like pineapple upside-down cake, while Spike went for the chocolate. There was one cake that caught Spike's fancy for obvious reasons—it was called Chocolate Spike and it bore a resemblance to her hairstyle.

But the picture that sent Spike's heart beating faster was that of a cake called Art Deco. It was beautiful and elegant—all dark chocolate inside, with a smooth white fondant surface, and classy accents of dark green and silver on top. A spray of calla lilies formed out of marzipan lay across the top and cascaded down one side. We oohed and aahed over it for a while, then Spike popped the question—"If I ever get married, will you make that cake for me?"

Friendship makes demands, but I wasn't sure that I could deliver on such a promise. I quickly calculated the odds of Spike ever tying the knot. She was thirty-six; there were no current contenders, but should one emerge, Spike just didn't seem to be the marrying kind. "Sure," I said.

During the two weeks that followed, those momentous changes in the other parts of the world began to unfold. And whatever confluence of stars and planets that set the peace dividend in motion, that same magic flowed from Eastern Europe, to South Africa, to San Francisco, where Spike met a man named Tom with long red hair and fell in love. She called me on the phone to tell me. I asked her if she would hold me to my promise. She said it wouldn't hurt to try a few practice cakes.

Spike and Tom's courtship progressed, aided no doubt by a few of Spike's own pies. And a year to the day of my foolish promise, she called again and asked me to stand up for her at her wedding the next August.

"Of course," said I, "but do I still have to make that cake?"

"Yes!"

Friendship must fulfill a promise, and Spike expected me to make good on mine. How could I, the Best Woman (we did away with the term Matron of Honor), deny the bride her wish? It took some time, but I managed to convince Spike that, lovely as that cake was, it just didn't fit her iconoclastic nature. What would? Pies, of course!

And so my role as the Best Woman came to mean taking care of the pie business. Little was required of me for the actual ceremony, which took place in court chambers, so all energy could be channeled into translating the wedding cake concept into pie. Should there be one big pie, big enough for a hundred guests? How would I ever bake it? Or a series of successively smaller pies, piled up in tiers? How would it not collapse under its own weight? Or a collection of regular-sized pies, creatively displayed? Possible.

Getting the pies was the easy part. Fifteen pies would be adequate, and twenty even better; I could bring five of them myself. Spike had a wealth of Pie Makers among her kith and kin and it wasn't hard to get the other fifteen lined up. Some of these Pie Makers would be driving a couple of hundred miles to come to this wedding. (There were some who would have driven around the world to see Spike get married.) So the ground rules were: only fruit pies; no eggs, milk, or cream; and bake the pie at the last possible moment before leaving. The challenge was to get twenty homemade pies from various parts of Minnesota, Wisconsin, and Iowa to Madison by August 26 in ninety-three-degree heat with equally high humidity and keep them fresh, unspoiled, and uncrushed. The Iowa Pie Makers broke some new ground here. They made their pies a week ahead of time, froze them unbaked, packed them in dry ice for the journey, then borrowed somebody's kitchen to bake them the night before. I led the Minnesota contingent with a newly designed pie box that had a rubber foam sheet in the bottom to keep the pie from sliding around and breaking its crust. Getting the pies was easy; figuring out how to arrange them was harder.

I rejected the idea of trying to stack the pies up in some sort of tier system—it just wouldn't work without crushing a great deal of good pie toward the bottom. Maybe I could create an illusion of tiers, but how? I went to the "maids" in search of help.

The "maids" are, regardless of actual gender, the helpful employees of the Maid of Scandinavia bakeware stores. A creative and knowledgeable bunch, they had solved more than a few baking problems for me before. I described the plan and they were intrigued. "Wedding pies!" they exclaimed. "How clever!" They had never heard of it ever being done before. However it turned out, they wanted photos of the event for their scrapbook. One of the "maids" came up with the answer: Raise up the center pie by putting a large circular pan of some height underneath the tablecloth, and place the others around the circumference—a simple and elegant solution that worked perfectly. I capped off the arrangement with one of their wedding cake ornaments.

Spike's friends were concerned about this man she was to marry. Was he good enough for her? Would he try to change her? Did he have enough substance to keep her interested? Did he like pie? I was the advance scout on this mission and I pronounced Spike and Tom not only well matched, but evenly matched. And as for pies, Tom's pedigree was impeccable. This marriage could work.

Friendship can deliver the goods. The wedding day arrived along with the Best Woman, best friends, and twenty of the best pies in the Midwest. Blueberry, cherry, apple, blackberry, rhubarb, raspberry, plum, apricot, even Spike's beloved grape pie. The vows exchanged, the service concluded, the couple and their guests adjourned to the feast. And on a table all their own stood an embarrassment of riches, the twenty pies in an artful arrangement of garlands of flowers and lace, and someone's thoughtful gift of an engraved pie server.

The cutting of a wedding cake is usually little more than a photo op. But with these pies, everyone stood around eating seconds and thirds, talking, mingling, marveling at the marriage of Spike and Tom and the widened vision we all now had of their lives. Someone said they should have exchanged vows right there, in front of the pies. Could there be a better witness to love and friendship? ⌒

18

◦ REST STOP ◦

MILE 297—
A SHIMMERING LIE

Pessimism is as American as apple pie—

frozen apple pie with a slice

of processed cheese.

—George F. Will

I don't know how long I've been driving. The maps are no help. The rules are outdated. It's late afternoon and the hunger for pie is wild. The road has those shiny lines at the horizon. You can't trust anything at this time of day, especially your own judgment. Must resist all urges to stop anywhere for

pie now. Must bypass all the siren songs, the mirages, the bill-
boards, the little voices that say truck stops have good pie
because that's where all the truckers go and they know where
the good food is. They don't. It's a lie. I turn on the car radio,
flip over a cassette, put in another CD, but all I get is Philip
Glass's score to *Koyaanisqatsi*. I take a detour. I get lost. The
road is just one long shimmering mirage. Maybe I've got it all
wrong. Maybe the pies aren't out there anymore. With the tank
close to empty and the road shimmering in heat, I resolve to
believe. One more try, just one more try. ∼

19

In a League of Our Own

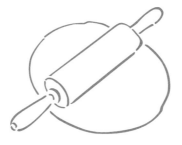

Statistics are to baseball what a
flaky crust is to Mom's apple pie.

—Harry Reasoner

I t's that time of year again, when I can't read a book review,
newspaper, or magazine without confronting one of Life's
Great Imponderables—baseball.

Something about spring does this. Bookstores set out
displays about this year's new crop of baseball books. Columnists
and commentators who never utter a sports metaphor begin to
wax eloquent about baseball. There's the predictable rash of
movies about baseball players I've never heard of. Many men I
know, and some women, get silly over this. For weeks on end I

sit on the outside of their company and conversation. They talk of nothing else but opening day, season tickets, brewskis, the team, ballpark franks, free agents, the demise of open-air stadiums, and the beauty of the game itself. (Beauty? Somebody needs to give me a clue.)

When April dawns in our fair state after gray, ugly March, I get excited about the first crocus, the first night I hear the peeper frogs singing their courtship in the muddy pond across the way, the first leaf of rhubarb I spy erupting from the ground. I look up to discover I am in the midst of people who speak a strange tongue, people who I swear I have known, worked with, had pleasant discourse with, who now align themselves with tribes I've never heard of. The anthropologist in me wants to study them, but the rest of me feels like one of life's great parades has passed me by.

I just don't get it. I use my gender as an excuse, lame though it may be. There were no Little League teams for girls when I was a tyke. Title IX made its debut after I started college. My brothers never played, nor my father, and if they ever took in a game, they didn't talk about it. I grew up singularly unexposed to America's favorite pastime. I don't know what it was we did, but it wasn't baseball. Now, when other mothers I know talk about their kids' T-ball games, I won't fess up to my ignorance. I really don't know what T-ball is. Really. Is it baseball? And what's the difference between baseball and softball, slow pitch and fast pitch? I don't know.

One time I thought about joining a women's city league. A bunch of women I worked with had a team together and invited me along. I tried it out one night but couldn't get beyond my innate ignorance of the game. Something about it bothered me, too—it seemed like the women were trying awfully hard to play a man's game rather than playing their own. I remember one woman, very earnest, trying very hard to explain some of the nuances of the game to me. She stooped down and began to draw a picture for me in the dirt. She laid out the next play for me and I nodded like the village idiot. She slapped me on the back, told me to "Go get 'em," then she hawked up a big gob and spat in the sand. That did it. It was like bad television and I wanted no part of it.

I have since given up trying to understand. I'm an old dog and baseball is a new trick. I've learned to mask my bewilderment with a few nods and polite small talk. I'm very happy as an expert in my own game, which as you know, dear Readers, is pie. Why try to be one of the guys when I'm captain of my own team and I've got season tickets to the most exciting game in town?

I could take the sports metaphor further, a lot further, but I won't because I hate sports metaphors almost as much as

I hate sports bars. And I'd be just as guilty as my women's softball teammates of trying to shape the richness of our lives into terms and standards defined by the guys.

But I would be wrong not to admit to some kinship between baseball and pie. Both are quintessentially American. Both are harbingers of spring. Both reveal the soul and beauty of not only the players but the fans. When spring arrives and normal law-abiding adults plan to cut work to catch opening day, I find myself playing hooky to stay home, cut the rhubarb, and enjoy the first pie of the season. It's really the same thing. And there is a special place where these seemingly disparate worlds overlap, where enthusiasm and appreciation for the game itself bubble over to create those icons of fandom—trading cards!

You may not have seen them yet because they aren't in circulation like baseball cards are, but Pie Maker Trading Cards will soon be making the rounds among collectors and traders. The format is the same: action photo on the front; portrait, narrative, and vital statistics on the back.

Here's a sampling of Pie Maker vital statistics and what they mean:

- **Lifetime Number of Pies**—a good-faith estimate of the number of pies made by each Pie Maker up to the current season. A few Pie Makers keep an actual count, marking crosshatches on a calendar, but that is not strictly necessary. Some feel this runs counter to the Pie Maker code of generosity, for it puts the emphasis in the wrong place. Still, it is a useful measure of experience and a count of at least a thousand is necessary to be inducted into the Hall of Fame.

- **Crust Ratio**—the number of parts of flour to the number of parts of shortening: 3 parts flour to 1 part shortening is the standard, but a 3.33 to 1 ratio is considered a little daring, and 2.5 to 1 is cheating.

- **Number of Blue Ribbons**—blue ribbons won at any state fair, county fair, or any other competition, as long as there are at least fifty entries. A low number or lack of blue ribbons does not always work against a Pie Maker. Some talented Pie Makers (see Helen Myhre's card on page 144) are too busy to enter contests or otherwise do not go in for competition.

- **August Quotient**—a complicated formula that expresses the relationship of heat and humidity to the total number of pies baked during August; used as an indicator of endurance, strength, and yield; numbers above 1 are admirable; anything much below .85 means you are having a bad season.

- **Personal Threshold**—the number of pies that can be made at any one time before Greatness is compromised; more is better.

- **Thanksgiving Day Lineup**—number of different pies served; more is better, but above six, your sanity is questioned.

- **Thickening Factor**—sometimes known as the "ooze factor," it is a formula that determines the amount of thickening used per cup of fruit. A factor of 2 means a slice will stand ramrod straight and salute. A factor of 1 means you might as well pour it in a glass and drink it. A number between 1.35 and 1.55 will give you just the right amount of ooze.

- **Generosity Index**—the most complicated measure of Pie Makers, it measures the volume of an average slice. The formula takes into consideration the diameter and depth of pies and the number of slices cut from the pie. It is an imperfect tool because it can be easily manipulated, yet it provides a way to observe the intent of a Pie Maker.

  Scores under 4.0 are not competitive, and those above 9.0 shouldn't be taken seriously. Most scores are clustered between 5.0 to 7.0, with the golden mean at 6.2. Most of the Queens of Pie and the All-Stars will have a Generosity Index between 6.5 and 8.0. A Pie Maker can handicap her score if she traditionally makes low-depth pies like raspberry or currant. Like all statistics, it's best not to look at this one on its own but in concert with the others.

There are leagues too, or the equivalent of leagues. We have three: the Liberal (custard, cream, and chocolate), the Conservative (fruit only and always a top crust), and the Crossover (all over the map). The All-Star team is called the Queens of Pie; each All-Star is inducted into a Hall of Fame after she has made at least a thousand pies in her lifetime.

Well, you can imagine the excitement this creates among collectors. Here are a couple of the hottest cards trading right now.

NITA SCHEMMEL

Lifetime Number of Pies	Crust Ratio	Number of Blue Ribbons	August Quotient
4,278	3:1.2	43	1.21
Personal Threshold	**Thanksgiving Day Lineup**	**Thickening Factor**	**Generosity Index**
10	6	1.46	7.1

Nita Schemmel, more widely known as one of the faces the Gedney Pickle company put on their jars, is also one of America's premier All-Star Pie Makers. Nita's fruit pies have a distinctive look: the top crust is pulled into a taut disk with no bumps, lumps, or wrinkles, modestly crimped, and tanned to perfection. It is the standard used by all judges at state fairs, and a standard few ever achieve. A native of Mankato, Minnesota, and true to her home state, Nita names the Haralson as her favorite pie apple. Well known for her encouragement of rookie Pie Makers, she's the Pie Maker most looked up to. When asked to share her secret on how to attain that perfect piecrust, she smiles and says, "Why, just follow the recipe on the back of the Crisco cans."

HELEN MYHRE

Lifetime Number of Pies	Crust Ratio	Number of Blue Ribbons	August Quotient
10,481!	3:.9	N/A	1.43
Personal Threshold	Thanksgiving Day Lineup	Thickening Factor	Generosity Index
24	9	1.3	7.4

Helen Myhre, an edges-first roller who always rolled for the Crossovers, is a true Queen of Pies. She has been an All-Star for many of her sixty-some pie baking years, having attained that magic number of a thousand pies sometime in her early twenties. An amateur until her mid-forties, she turned professional when she opened up the Norske Nook in Osseo, Wisconsin. She sold the business in 1991 but hasn't retired from making pies; far from it, she still turns out at least twenty-eight pies every week for her son's restaurant. Helen popularized the midwestern classic sour cream–raisin pie for thousands of hungry travelers on I-94, who until then thought of Wisconsin only in terms of cheese.

And my favorite trading card:

ANNE DIMOCK

Lifetime Number of Pies	Crust Ratio	Number of Blue Ribbons	August Quotient
643	3:1	2	1.073
Personal Threshold	Thanksgiving Day Lineup	Thickening Factor	Generosity Index
8	5	1.5	7.2

Anne Dimock, 1998 Rookie of the Year for the Conservatives, is a center-outward roller who prefers her ten-pound solid oak rolling pin over any other. Anne is a daughter of Mary Dimock, an All-Star Pie Maker from the Great Swamp of New Jersey. Although she has yet to win any state fair blue ribbons, she has shown extraordinary improvement in her scores over recent years and seems destined to take home the "big one" this year if she enters her rhubarb. She comes from a long line of Pie Makers and aspires to become a Queen of Pies like her mother and grandmothers before her. Her favorite pie apples betray her Yankee origins: McIntosh, closely followed by Cortland.

My action photo shows me with a crust delicately draped over my behemoth rolling pin, ready to flip it on top of an apple pie. The portrait shot zooms in to catch me pensive and reflective, with a cornucopia of fruit in my arms. I love it—it is so *me*!

So how do you get hold of Pie Maker Trading Cards? You won't find them in sports memorabilia shops, nor at swap meets—not yet anyway. No, you have to patronize the places where they make and serve real pies. You have to get to know the Pie Maker herself before she will grace you with one of her cards. You must prepare yourself and show that you are ready by discussing ooze factors and crust ratios. You must be able to recite the statistics for the last ten seasons for Nita Schemmel, Helen Myhre, Lola Nebel, and your mother. You have to lament the demise of real pies the same way men keen for the loss of open-air stadiums. But lacking all that, you can try this . . .

If you bake them, they will come.

20
THE POLITICS OF PIE

No man's pie is freed from

his ambitious finger.

—William Shakespeare, *King Henry VIII*

J ust when you thought it was safe to open the newspaper
again, when there couldn't be anything left to politicize,
and when the nation just might be on the mend after the
last presidential election, another soul-rattling divisiveness
comes upon the land . . . the politics of pie.

Pie culture, although relatively free from insurgency, is
deeply political. Its battles and disputes are quiet and sane and
may go unnoticed by most of us. But its still, deep waters are

parted by two great debates: What constitutes a True Pie? And, as always, who will get the biggest piece of it?

Ever the activists, Pie Makers caucus at the county fair. They meet in kitchen cabinets around the country. They hold their state convention each year in August at the state fair. And what Washington, D.C., is to other politicians, Cincinnati, Ohio, is to Pie Makers—the home of Procter & Gamble, makers of Crisco. There is no constitution—we are not a nation unto ourselves—but we tend to favor parliamentary representation rather than a two-party system. As in other political arenas, things pretty much line up along conservative-moderate-liberal lines with fringe groups at each end. And, sadly, we are not above pork pie politics.

Pie politics has its own divisive issues. Among Pie Makers, you are either pro-choice or pro-crust. This refers to whether you insist all pies have a top crust, or whether you can choose meringue, crumb, whipped cream, nuts, a regular top crust, or no crust at all. Another raging issue is whether one can use ready-made piecrusts and still call oneself a Pie Maker. There are big-money interests behind this one—Procter & Gamble lobbies heavily against the prepared piecrusts. The Pillsbury/General Mills coalition lobbies for them, calling them the moral property of women. Me? I'm a pro-crustinator; I think we should make prepared piecrusts safe and available, but I don't think anyone should use them.

I am a pie conservative. I never knew I was a pie conservative, indeed I hadn't had my pie political consciousness raised, until I read an article by Sue Hubbell in the *New Yorker* magazine. Sue Hubbell, our movement's pioneer and visionary, described her cross-country search for real pies. On an ecumenical mission, she ate and enjoyed pies of all kinds. She came upon a gentleman in Indiana who referred to himself as a pie conservative: he never touched pies with cream or eggs in them. It was like reading the symptoms of my own particular disease for the first time, discovering that there is a name for it and that there are others out there like me.

The conservative platform rides on what constitutes a True Pie. A True Pie is fresh fruit that is lightly bound up to capture its juices in a soft ooze, sweet enough only to keep you from puckering, and spiced subtly only to accentuate the fruit's own flavor. And—most important of all—it lies between *two* crusts of amazing architectural interest—delicacy and dryness, with strength enough to hold it all in. (This also reminds me of the perfect man.)

I have never recognized anything other than a fruit pie as a True Pie. Apple, blueberry, blackberry, peach, mincemeat, raisin, plum, cherry, all other berries, pear, and cranberry all qualify as real pies according to my orthodoxy. My beloved rhubarb does too, even though I know it has the same relationship to a true fruit as broccoli does. It tastes like fruit, so I say it's okay. Many of us split on pecan and pumpkin. The historical deconstructionists allow them, but the rest of us don't. What I'll never understand is how there came to be pies made out of custard.

Chocolate pie, banana cream pie, sour cream–raisin pie, lemon meringue pie, key lime pie, coconut cream, French silk (what *is* that anyway?), butterscotch pie—where did these come from and how dare they call themselves pies?

I used to be a pie bigot, part of an ultraconservative faction, but their activism became too extreme for me. They would organize around a call for a return to traditional pie values. Fine, but then they demanded that certain cookbooks be removed from the library shelves. My views moderated when they began to burn custard pies on the lawns of astonished home owners. I admit the rise of those custard and whipped cream things at the expense of the True Pie still threatens me. I have not embraced multiculturalism in pies, nor am I likely to. I am of an old school, a pie WASP and a blue blood. I come from a long line of Pie Makers, a true Daughter of the American Revolution. I am not about to change. I don't want to.

And yet . . . there is something about a row of custard pies, sitting there just being what they are and nothing else, each one a bridge to unknown territory. I had a pie like that beckon to me once. It was in the Norske Nook in Osseo, Wisconsin, where they turn out seventy-four pies every day, most of them cream or custard. Their best seller is sour cream–raisin pie, but that wasn't the one I caught flirting with me. It was the butterscotch pie. Across a crowded room, it caught my eye and locked me in. Bereft of a top crust, it looked positively naked, I thought. That soft brown filling and real whipped cream had enough moxie to stand up and be counted among the True Pies. Pretty soon I wasn't sure I could live without trying it, and so I did, breaking all my own rules about when and where and what types of pies to eat.

It's hard to drop all prejudices, very hard, but one slipped away that day. I remain among the party faithful but sometimes I wander to where experience chips away at belief. It is not in the nature of Pie Makers, even conservatives, to resort to protectionism. Let the market decide whether cream pies or True Pies are to reign! Old rivalries die hard, but die they must—laissez-faire must give way to détente. Do we really want a pie buildup, three fruit pies for every one of custard, each side poised with first-strike capability?

Or should we get on with the important business, the Realpolitik, of dividing up the pie for all of us? ∼

21

● REST STOP ●

MILE 327–BRAHAM, MINNESOTA

I think it's another mirage and don't trust what I see. There, on the corner of Main and Route 60, on the south side of the red-brick building, is a larger-than-life mural of pies, fruit, and coffee cups in beautiful colors. Is this a hallucination? Where could I be? I'm in Braham, Minnesota, where every day is pie day.

I don't remember how I got here. One moment I was dizzy and lost, and in the next I stood in front of the Tusen Tack thrift store and Park Café in Braham. Perhaps the road rolled up over me and then unraveled, leaving me precisely where I needed to be. Some roads can do that.

The Park Café had homemade pies, beautiful, delicious pies made from scratch by people who've done this for years. Apple, lemon meringue, peach. Cherry, pecan, chocolate. All the old standards and a couple of new ones. For decades, people on the way to their lake cabins up north stopped in Braham for their coffee break and a piece of pie. The Park never stopped making pies the old-fashioned way and never attained the tourist status that could jeopardize their integrity. Braham remains a bit out of the way except for one day of the year—the first Friday in August—when the town fills to overflowing with visitors. That day is Braham Pie Day and it celebrates all things pie.

It's a remarkable occasion. Over five hundred home-made pies for sale, pie contests, a pie anthem, pie books, pie ties, pie-ku poetry, pie this and pie that. Silly? Only a little. Braham Pie Day shows off the lighthearted tip of a massive iceberg of community pride and cohesion. Braham chose the pie as its emblem, its symbol to the world of who it is and what it believes in. Braham gets it. It celebrates its Pie Makers and nurtures the next generation that will take their place. Braham takes responsibility for creating a culture that holds up against popular entertainment and new media. Self-determination through pie!

Braham Pie Day is the one day out of the year when everything relates to pie. But Braham, the community, spends the rest of the year remembering how pie shapes its life. Every difficult crust and runny fruit has a corollary. Every success and pie contest winner has examples they followed. Every pie made throughout the year, at the Park Café, the school cafeteria, or in home kitchens, has a place on a string of pearls that extends backward and forward in time. Every person in Braham has a role in the passion play, the folklore, the myth, and the fable that is pie. Every day is pie day in Braham, Minnesota. ∿

22
THE QUEEN IS DEAD—
LONG LIVE THE QUEEN!

There in the dark with the lights all out,

And your sleepless mind seems

    to jump about,

What would come right back

    before your eyes,

Was mother's love with her cake and pies.

—John L. Sanders, "Mother's Cakes and Pies"

I was asleep when the call came. I let the phone ring, thinking it was a wayward call from a fax machine. The answering machine clicked on, then nothing. Silence. Half a minute later the phone rang again. This time I answered. It was my sister with the news. "Bad news," she said. "Mom died."

It happened quickly. An abdominal aortic aneurysm burst and she died before hitting the floor. She was eighty-one years old. The Path of a Thousand Pies ended abruptly for my mother. We'd last spoken a few days before over the telephone. A lively conversation, it left us both happy. It was August and it was hot and humid in both Florida and Minnesota.

Death may not have its own season, but it has its own rituals and protocol. It's bad enough losing a mother, but a Queen? We began preparations for her state funeral. I asked my father if I could write the obituary and he said yes. I labored over her brief biography; how to tell the story of a life in just a couple of column inches? How do I say that she walked the Path of a Thousand Pies, that she was called to apple pie, that she contributed the critical mass of pies necessary to get the Pie Renaissance off the ground? How can I begin to make the world understand the loss they suffered? So I wrote the obituary several times and decided in the end to capture her world of pies in one brief sentence. But it was enough. Everyone who knew her understood, and those who didn't were intrigued enough to find out. A reporter for the big Miami paper called after reading the obituary in the smaller local paper. Caught by the pie reference, they wanted to expand it into a story. So that's how my mother, "MARY DIMOCK, PIE MAKER, DEAD AT 81" came to appear on the "Deaths Elsewhere" page alongside former entertainment, sports, and diplomatic luminaries.

My father was there to greet me as I got off the plane in Florida. His eyes met mine but then quickly noticed something else. He smiled big and warm at the pie basket I carried. I unloaded the pies in his kitchen, then stole away for a secret errand. Later that night, after the rest of the family arrived, we gathered for a quick buffet dinner in my parents' dining room. We all expected to see Mary walk into the room at every moment, and we said it frequently as if that would make it so. There were thirteen of us and it was good that I'd made the two apple pies. We ate them up that night as brothers and sisters and father and cousins laughed, reminisced, cried a little, and called forth memory after memory of Mary and her pies and her life. The Paula Reds were perfect, the crusts dry and flaky, and for one more time we were together. This was the eulogy I intended.

The funeral was in the Catholic church my mother had attended ever since she'd moved to Florida. She was well known and loved there too. As a family we asked for no flowers and encouraged donations to a charity instead, but there was one large flower arrangement at the foot of the altar—a beautiful array of sunflowers and other summer blooms emerging from an opened pie basket. Wonder how that got there. Her service coincided with the feast of the Ascension of Mary into Heaven, a holy day of obligation in the Catholic Church. The Ascension praises Mary the Mother of Jesus as she is raised into heaven on a cloud, already a blessed saint. The similarity was not lost on anybody. So it should not come as a surprise that there was a miracle. Well, the Catholic Church probably won't classify it as a true miracle, and they'll appoint a commission to investigate and later debunk it as a hysterical apparition of mourners, but none of that matters because we know what we saw. The service was the full Catholic Mass complete with sermon, offertory, and Holy Communion. In that moment of supreme transformation when the priest raised the Eucharist above his head, the white, round host flickered, then grew and shimmered and turned golden tan and began to revolve, completing three full turns before it returned to its original state. And the church filled with a delicious sweet aroma, less like incense, more like cinnamon.

Some unusual weather was reported in New Jersey that day. Cyclonic winds tore apples from their branches, but instead of finding heaps of damaged fruit under the trees,

bruised, rotting, and covered with wasps, orchardists found—
nothing. Elsewhere there were reports of large dark hail or
meteor showers. Thousands of mysterious compost heaps with
lots of apple seeds sprang up overnight like fairy ring mushrooms.
And after the cacophony of these unusual disturbances lit up
police switchboards, a period of equally unusual calm moved in
for about a week. No one could explain it but there just wasn't
much crime that week.

Some years before my mother's death, my father had
received a similar phone call. "I'm sorry, Mr. Dimock, your
mother passed away a few hours after you left." GeeGee had
been in a nursing home after breaking a hip. She was ninety-
nine years old. She died of old age. There was an early spring
that year, no late frosts, and all the fruit trees thrived.

And several years after my mother's death, Carla
Kingstad, my mother-in-law, died after a long illness. She
was seventy-one. There was an especially late harvest of blueberries that year; people were picking blueberries all the way
through November.

They are all gone now, the great pie lineage severed.
The Queens of Pies are dead. Of course it takes a loss to

understand what one has. Or had. Security is knowing there is some more pie left. But at some point you realize that you are on the downside of a full plate of pie. There are limits to how long this business of life can go on, for once we are born, our natural cycles rush us headlong toward certain deterioration. When the last piece of pie disappears, it's like losing a good friend. That wonderful crust—gone. The sweet pure fruit— gone. Nothing left but that damn empty pie tin and the longing. And when it ends, it's all over. And it's about as easy as pie.

The Queens of Pie Are Dead—
Long Live the Queens!

Edna Voorhees Dimock (1878–1978)
Mary Maag Dimock (1915–1997)
Carla Bell Kingstad (1930–2002)

23

MILE 360—FULL CIRCLE

I ate umble pie with an appetite.

—Charles Dickens, *David Copperfield*

W ell, here we are, back where we started—our Pie Ramble comes full circle. Between a disappointing beginning and a hopeful finish we found evidence that pie is in decline but not extinct. The expansive and generous side of people unfailingly seeks out good pie and finds it, but it was a tough road there for a while. The loss of good pies in our lives is lamentable on its own, but when I think about how it may forecast an even greater calamity—like the canary in the coal mine—I really worry. I can make my own pies, I can make them for my family and my friends, but this is a big pie-less world for most people.

In spite of the recipes and tips on technique, making a pie comes down to three steps. The first step is memory, the second is resolve, and the third is the doing.

I've brought you through the portals of the first two and now you stand on the threshold of the third. The Pie Renaissance needs more artisans to weave pies back into our fabric. Just tell yourself it's like tying a shoelace. It looks like a complicated knot, but you just make a few loops and tug them into place. Eventually, that's how making a pie will feel to you, like tying a shoelace, riding a bike, or reciting a poem from heart. So go back to that time within you when you learned to do these things. Roll back the apprehension, the doubt, and enter the childlike state of grace where all things are possible and anything lost can be found again. The pie you seek resides not only in memory and imagination—your next piece of pie begins right here. ∼

EPILOGUE

After finishing a piece of great pie, you always wish there was just a little bit more, one more mouthful to savor or linger over. It seems the Queen of Pies left a little morsel behind. I found it the day after the funeral, before leaving Florida to return home with my now-empty pie basket. A pie—the last pie made by Mary Dimock. It was blueberry and it lay frozen and unbaked in the freezer in her kitchen. Maybe she knew she was going and that she'd need to leave something to ease the transition of our loss of her. Maybe this was just another pie, like the thousand and more before this one, squirreled away like something for a rainy day. What to do with it? Surely it was raining now.

No shortage of good ideas—donate it to the Smithsonian, bake and eat it right now, give it a new home in my empty pie basket—but we left it right there in the freezer. One thing we did know for sure was that she had made this pie for her husband of fifty-three years. The last pie of Mary Dimock should stay in frozen suspension in Florida until my father was ready to do something with it.

And that day came a couple of months later. He telephoned me to talk a little bit. And I remember thinking how strange and new it was for him to do the calling and talking. Just before the logical end of the conversation, for he would always be a logical man, he asked me, "How do I bake that frozen pie?"

Don't thaw the pie—bake it straight from the freezer.

Preheat the oven to 425 degrees. Cut several vents in the top crust with a small, sharp knife. Bake it at 425 for 20 minutes. Turn the oven down to 350 degrees and bake for 30 minutes, until you see a little dribble of blueberry juice coming out of a vent.

"I think I can handle that," he said. Old dogs can learn new tricks. And at age eighty-two, my father baked his first pie.

First the crust of melting sand

Then waves of fruit and juice

Some crumbs—all done